The odd marks of punctuation in Emily Dickinson's manuscripts have puzzled scholars for years. Professor Edith Wylder, a pioneer in the field of Dickinson scholarship, noticed in the course of her research that the four distinctive phonetic marks used in Ebenezer Porter's *Rhetorical Reader,* which was used at Amherst Academy while Emily Dickinson studied there, discusses the marks for rising, falling, high-low, and monotone vocal patterns. Her theory is that Emily Dickinson used the elocution marks systematically to record on paper what she heard in her own ear as she wrote the poems. ("The ear is the last face," said the poet in a letter to Thomas Wentworth Higginson.) Professor Wylder also links this punctuation practice and Emily Dickinson's capitalization with the diacritical symbols of modern linguists and the typographical efforts of contemporary poets to visualize the sound qualities of inflection, stress, and juncture.

With the elaboration of this theory, which has already elicited great interest from poets like John Ciardi and Charles Tomlinson, the author sheds important light on Dickinson's metrics and, especially where the phonetic analysis is allowed to supervene upon the metric analysis, offers new and sometimes radically different interpretations of some of her most difficult poems. The Introduction to this edition of Emily Dickinson's manuscript poems enlarges on and clarifies a widely misinterpreted article that Professor Wylder wrote for *Saturday Review* on March 30, 1963 (under the name of Edith Perry Stamm).

The Last Face

THE
LAST FACE

Emily Dickinson's
Manuscripts

BY

EDITH WYLDER

Albuquerque
UNIVERSITY OF NEW MEXICO PRESS

Poems 89, 130, 165, 177, 239, 249, 252, 280, 311, 328, 338, 341, 412, 441, 449, 465, 480, 510, 512, 520, 621, 709, 712, 754, 810, 861, 986, 1052, 1068, 1072, 1084, 1463, 1551, 1554, 1587:
Reprinted by permission of the publishers and the Trustees of Amherst College from Thomas H. Johnson, Editor, THE POEMS OF EMILY DICKINSON, Cambridge, Mass.: The Belknap Press of Harvard University Press, Copyright, 1951, 1955, by The President and Fellows of Harvard College.

First Edition

FOR DEB

Acknowledgments

There is no difficulty knowing where to begin in expressing my gratitude to those who have helped me with this work. I am most deeply indebted to George Arms, not only for his rigorous and imaginative direction of the original dissertation from which this book grew, but for the inspiration and guidance he has provided for many years. I am particularly indebted also to Franklin Dickey and Morris Freedman for their perceptive critical comments and for their indispensable encouragement along the way. Because of the immediate and affirmative responses of Charles Anderson, Stanley Burnshaw, and John Ciardi, my theory was given its first public airing in *Saturday Review* in 1963. Considerable encouragement toward the idea of a selected edition such as this was given me by Charles Tomlinson, and to him I owe many thanks for his suggestions and for his help in paving the way for future publication.

A grant of travel funds from the University of New Mexico and further assistance from my father enabled me to do the necessary firsthand research on the Dickinson manuscripts in the Harvard collection at the Houghton Library and in the Higginson collection at the Boston Public Library in the summer of 1963; and the Department of English at the University of New Mexico purchased the microfilm of the Bingham collection at Amherst College for my further research.

To Dr. William H. Bond, director, and to Miss Carolyn Jakeman and the staff of the Houghton Library I owe a special debt

Contents

The low falling slide (ˌ) has been inadvertently omitted from its proper position under the last letter of these words on the following pages:

> p. 10, l. 12 ("word")
> p. 11, last line ("word")
> p. 24, l. 27, Lark
> p. 44, l. 15, Lark
> p. 69, l. 22 (word)
> p. 84, poem 441, l. 3, told
> p. 85, poem 465, l. 3, Air
> p. 91, poem 709, l. 7, Creator
> p. 106, l. 1, Lark

Miscellaneous marks omitted or in error on the following pages:

> p. 76, poem 239, l. 4, me! (exclamation point has a line at its base)
> p. 80 (see overleaf for reprint of page)
> p. 94, poem 861, l. 1, Lark (rising slide should be low falling slide)

To Stump, and Stack, and Stem,
A Summer's empty Room -
Acres of Joints, where Harvests were,
Recordless   but for them -

It Ruffles Wrists of Posts
As Ankles of a Queen -
Then stills it's Artisans   like Ghosts -
Denying they have been,

Manuscript: About 1862 (H 278). The copy is signed "Emily -".

Other manuscripts: A semifinal draft, written earlier in the same year, is in packet 29 (H 155a). A variant twelve-line version (Bingham 98-4B-3) was written about 1864, and in 1883, a copy of this later version was sent to Thomas Niles (Bingham 106-32).

328

A Bird came down the Walk -
He did not know I saw -
He bit an Angleworm in halves
And ate the fellow,   raw,

And then he drank a Dew
From a convenient Grass,
And then hopped sidewise to the Wall
To let a Beetle pass -

He glanced with rapid eyes
That hurried all around,
They looked like frightened Beads,   I thought,
He stirred his Velvet Head

of gratitude for their courteous assistance during my examination of the manuscripts, for their help in procuring photostats of the poems, and for the kind permission of the Harvard College Library to transcribe from the manuscripts in the Houghton collection for this book. I am indebted to Dr. J. Richard Phillips of the Amherst College Library for the kind permission of the Trustees of Amherst College to transcribe from the manuscripts in the Bingham collection. My thanks go also to Dr. Charles R. Green of the Jones Library in Amherst for sending me a copy of the Amherst Academy catalogues and of Frederick Tuckerman's *History* of the Academy, and to the librarians at the University of New Mexico and Utah State University for their help in obtaining the now rare Porter's *Rhetorical Reader*. Mr. Newton F. McKeon of the Converse Library at Amherst College was kind enough to make the necessary arrangements for purchasing the microfilm of the Bingham collection. My publisher and I particularly wish to thank Mr. Mark Carroll, director of the Harvard University Press, for his very courteous permission to reprint the poems of Emily Dickinson that appear in this book. To the text edited by Thomas H. Johnson I have added the diacritical marks from the manuscripts, and I have indicated in footnotes each instance in which I have changed Mr. Johnson's text.

I am also indebted to my several friends and colleagues who have responded enthusiastically to my project over the last few years, and whose sympathy and indulgence have allowed me to work out many problems. In particular I should like to thank Mary Alice Matthews of the Instructional Resources Center at Southwest Minnesota State College for her painstaking rendering of the diacritical marks in the text of the poems. Finally, I owe my very special thanks to my husband Delbert for his invaluable assistance with the explications and for the understanding that has made the completion of this book possible.

Wild nights – Wild nights!
Were I with thee
Wild nights – should be
Our luxury!

Futile – the winds –
to a Heart in port –
Done with the Compass –
Done with the Chart –!

Rowing in Eden –
Ah, the Sea!
Might I but moor –
Tonight –
In thee!

---

x x x

I died for Beauty - but
was scarce
Adjusted in the Tomb
When One who died for
truth, was lain
In an Adjoining Room -

He questioned softly "Why I
failed"?
"For Beauty -", I replied -
"And I - for truth - Themself
are One -
We Bretheren, are," He said -

And so, as Kinsmen, met
a Night -
We talked between the Rooms -
Until the Moss had reached
our lips
And covered up - Our names -

After great pain, a formal
feeling comes –
the Nerves sit ceremonious,
like tombs –
the stiff Heart questions was
it He, that bore,
And "Yesterday, or Centuries before"?

the Feet, mechanical, go round –
Of Ground, or Air, or Ought –
A Wooden way
Regardless grown,
A Quartz contentment, like
a stone –

this is the Hour of Lead –
Remembered, if outlived,
As Freezing persons, recollect
the Snow –
First – Chill – then Stupor – then
the letting go –

I read my sentence - steadily -
Reviewed it with my eyes,
To see that I made no
mistake
In it's extremest Clause -
the Date, and manner, of the
shame -
And then the Pious Form
that "God have mercy" on the Soul
the Jury voted Him -
I made my soul familiar with her extremity
that - at the last, it should not
be a novel Agony -
But She, and Death, acquainted -
Meet tranquilly, as friends -
Salute, and pass, without a Hint -
And there, the Matter ends -

INTRODUCTION

The Manuscript Notations

"The Ear is the last Face. We hear after we see. Which to tell you first is still my Dismay." [1] This is Emily Dickinson's statement to Thomas Wentworth Higginson. It is at the center of her poetic manifesto, which she incorporated at artful random into her letters to the man she acknowledged as her literary preceptor. Written over a hundred years ago, Emily Dickinson's private declaration is echoed today in a public manifesto by Charles Olson in *The New American Poetry*.

> From the moment the projective purpose of the act of verse is recognized, the content does—it will—change. If the beginning and the end is breath, voice in its largest sense, then the material of verse shifts. It has to.[2]

Since the material of verse begins with the written word, the poet's task of "shifting" that material necessarily involves bridging the gap between the written language and its life source,

[1] *The Letters of Emily Dickinson*, eds. Thomas H. Johnson and Theodora Ward (Cambridge, Mass.: The Belknap Press of Harvard University Press, 1965), II, 528; hereafter cited as *Letters*. The punctuation in this and in all quotations from Emily Dickinson's letters follows that of the printed text, not of the manuscripts.

[2] *The New American Poetry*, ed. Donald Allen (New York: Grove Press, 1960), p. 394.

1

the spoken language. The marks of punctuation normally serve as one such bridge, symbolizing, in part at least, certain rhetorical patterns of speech. But for the projective purposes of many twentieth-century poets (e. e. cummings serves as a particularly good example) the conventional system of punctuation has proved inadequate and has been supplemented by a strategic use of typography. A century ago such strategy would have been impossible for the poet composing in longhand. But for Emily Dickinson, whose concern with projection was equally as strong as that of any poet today, the standard elocutionary symbols of her day provided a means of accomplishing much the same purpose. The contemporary poets' typographical innovations are recorded in the printed text of their work, but few readers today have had the opportunity to study Emily Dickinson's work in the form in which she set it down. Several scholars who have studied the manuscripts have either failed to recognize the consistency of her rhetorical punctuation or have not looked beyond its source in nineteenth-century elocution to recognize its full poetic function.

The Controversy

In 1963 I presented my theory of the rhetorical basis of the manuscript notations in a brief article for the *Saturday Review*,[3] hoping to remove the last shadow of technical inconsistency and imprecision cast by the transcribed "dashes" and "commas" of the Harvard variorum text.[4] These findings, however, have been misinterpreted to the extent that the shadow may instead have been darkened. It is time then to clarify matters by making some important distinctions between the nineteenth-century

[3] Edith Perry Stamm, "Emily Dickinson: Poetry and Punctuation," *Saturday Review*, XLVI (March 30, 1963), 26–27, 74.

[4] *The Poems of Emily Dickinson*, ed. Thomas H. Johnson (Cambridge, Mass.: The Belknap Press of Harvard University Press, 1958); hereafter cited as *Poems of Dickinson*.

elocutionists' use of their symbols and Emily Dickinson's use; to look briefly at the poet's notational system from the standpoint of certain principles of contemporary linguistics; to examine it closely in relation to the poetry it punctuates; and finally to let the punctuation speak for itself in the text of her work.

I had said that Dickinson's unique notational system was rooted in nineteenth-century elocution, particularly those principles and symbols in Porter's *Rhetorical Reader*,[5] the standard elocution text listed in the Amherst Academy catalogues for the years that the poet was a student there, and that the essential function of her punctuation was to "direct the reading" of her work. Taking "reading" to mean "declaiming" only, some scholars have regrettably concluded that the rhetorical theory implies that the poet placed the notations in the lines of her work simply to ensure its proper oral recitation. For example, Theodora Ward, co-editor of the Harvard *Letters*, responding to my article, stated that "It is hard to imagine Emily urgently asking for help and at the same time dictating to her correspondent how to read her letter to an audience." [6]

In my reply to Mrs. Ward I indicated that Emily Dickinson's "synthesis of rhetorical notation and grammatical punctuation" should not be interpreted as "simply directing the reading of her lines 'to an audience' "; rather, the poet "was punctuating in a far more subtle sense than any of her elocution tutors or earlier readers would have dreamed." [7] Apparently my stress on the "synthesis" was not strong enough, for several scholars have since neglected to make the necessary distinction between "read-

[5] Ebenezer Porter, *The Rhetorical Reader* (New York: Mark H. Newman, 1835); hereafter cited as *Reader*.
[6] In a Letter to the Editor, *Saturday Review*, XLVI (April 27, 1963), p. 25. The letter I had cited refers to one of Emily Dickinson's to T. W. Higginson.
[7] *Ibid.* (May 25, 1963), p. 23.

ing" and "reading aloud" in confronting the rhetorical theory.[8]

To be sure, her notations imply that the poet was concerned with "proper reading," but only as it relates to the way we understand what we read—specifically in terms of tone—not as it may incidentally relate to the way the same material is presented orally. There is no reason to suppose that Emily Dickinson understood otherwise. She was concerned that her written lines were "alive," that they "breathed," [9] that they communicated her meaning as fully and precisely and with the same sense of immediacy *as if* she had spoken them. That is the point. Her punctuation system is an integral part of her attempt to create in written form the precision of meaning inherent in the tone of the human voice.

"The Ear is the last Face. We hear after we see." Obviously, the poet's reference is to written, not oral, communication, and the emphasis on hearing suggests her understanding of the importance of tone as the final determinant of meaning. The way we hear what we read—in the mind's ear, of course—is the crucial factor in our understanding; it is "the last Face." But the written language is traditionally not constructed to delineate the variety or overtones of the meaning possible in actual speech. For example, in the spoken language, the simple phrase "I love you" can convey any one of several different meanings, depending on the particular stresses, pauses, and inflections the speaker uses. The writer is normally far more limited. This was Emily Dickinson's "Dismay," and her unique punctuation

---

[8] See, for example, the questions appended to a reprint of my *Saturday Review* article in *14 by Emily Dickinson*, ed. Thomas M. Davis (Chicago: Scott, Foresman and Co., 1964), p. 161; an article entitled "Emily Dickinson's Punctuation," by Brita Lindberg in *Studia Neophilologica*, XXXVII (1965), 327–359; R. W. Franklin's discussion in *The Editing of Emily Dickinson: A Reconsideration* (Madison, Milwaukee and London: University of Wisconsin Press, 1967), pp. 118–128; and Ruth Miller's comments in *The Poetry of Emily Dickinson* (Middletown, Connecticut: Wesleyan University Press, 1968), pp. 34–35.

[9] *Letters*, II, 403.

system became one of her means for bridging the communications gap, of lending to the written language much of that precision of tone, that "breath" of meaning, otherwise possible only in speech.

As we shall see, Emily Dickinson's system employs some of the symbols of the nineteenth-century elocutionists and displays a good deal of the contemporary linguists' understanding of speech characteristics. But it is not meant to direct actual speech or to describe it scientifically, for it is essentially a poetic device, to be understood in those terms. In a sense her notations work upon the mind's ear in much the same way a poetic image works upon the mind's eye. Normally the image creates an impression of the actual experience by attempting to define its essence in terms of a particular part. It does not describe the total experience because, of course, it could not. Working with and within the lines they punctuate, Emily Dickinson's notations register upon the mind's ear only those vocal intonations which are essential to define or particularize the tone of the lines. They are, then, not directions or descriptions of voice, but *impressions* of voice.

The oral interpreter, like any other reader, will be concerned with the punctuation of Emily Dickinson's lines only as it serves to sharpen his understanding of their meaning. That understanding, not the punctuation, will direct his own reinterpretation.

The general misunderstanding of the rhetorical theory is probably a result of my emphasis in the original *Saturday Review* article upon the great popularity of oral recitation during Emily Dickinson's school days. This was, I'm afraid, an unfortunate emphasis, but it was intended to show that the poet's adoption of some of the basic elocutionary symbols for her punctuation system was understandable in the light of the broad interest in literary expression in her day and of her own direct experience with it. A glance through any of the popular school readers of Dickinson's time will attest to the importance placed upon oral recitation. Clifton Johnson lists "the art of speaking" as one of the standard courses of the more than 100 academies operating in Massachusetts after 1840.[10] And George Whicher, in his biography, says:

> Literary expression was as vital a part of education in the 1840's as scientific attainments. The more ambitious college students not only submitted to the discipline of rhetorical exercises throughout the four years of their course, but strove to advance their skill in speaking and writing by taking part in the programs of rival literary societies and of the Greek-letter fraternities. They even organized, in addition, small private groups to hear and criticize their essays and orations. Public exhibitions were frequent and were commonly well attended. People flocked in from the surrounding countryside to attend the free show. The Academy was quite as active as the College in this way. Its pupils were expected to write compositions once a fortnight and read them on Wednesday afternoons. None of Emily's compositions have survived, but one of her teachers in his old age recalled them as extraordinary for their brilliance and originality. She was not singular, however, in possessing a highly developed faculty of expression. Boys and girls vied with each other to win the approbation of their teachers and fellow students, and whatever laurels Emily won were achieved in the face of keen competition.[11]

This kind of evidence, however, was originally presented to support the assumption that Emily Dickinson was well enough

[10] Clifton Johnson, *Old Time Schools and School Books* (New York: The Macmillan Company, 1904).
[11] George Whicher, *This Was a Poet* (Ann Arbor: University of Michigan Press, 1957), pp. 48–49.

acquainted with the symbols used by the elocutionists to have adopted and modified some of them for her own purposes, and that her elocutionary training would have helped to impress upon her the importance of poetry's oral quality. Moreover, she could easily have assumed that her simplified system of punctuation, which used the four standard inflectional notations of all the major nineteenth-century elocutionists, would be understood by most of her contemporaries because they too would have been exposed to the basic precepts of elocution either directly in the classroom or indirectly through the very popular community performances.

In her original criticism Mrs. Ward was concerned that although Emily Dickinson's punctuation seems "fairly consistent," her use of the marks "varied considerably at different periods in her life," and that the "greatest use of the 'dashes' that appear in the Harvard edition were those of the greatest stress in her life, both as woman and poet"—for instance, the letter to Higginson which I had cited "contained 28 marks of this kind." When the notations can be understood to function as a *substitute* punctuation which serves a grammatical as well as a rhetorical purpose, it should not be difficult to see how the notations function as a controlling force, setting off the tightly compressed phrasing. Since there is a general correspondence in Dickinson's writing between the degree of compression and the intensity of the emotion, there will usually be a similar correspondence between the number of "dashes" and the degree of emotional intensity expressed.

Transcribing the Notations

One final element of the general controversy over the viability of the rhetorical theory needs to be considered before the theory is explained in full. This has to do with the editing of the notations. Because they are unorthodox and their distribution is

seemingly erratic, Mrs. Ward indicated that no two editors
could agree on a consistent method of reproducing them in
print. At this point, then, I should like to outline briefly the
technical basis for the editing of the notations in this text. First,
every manuscript of poetry and many of the letters in the
Dickinson collection at the Houghton Library, the Bingham
collection in the Amherst College Library (on microfilm), and
the Higginson collection in the Boston Public Library were
carefully examined to arrive at a general basis for categorizing
the notations. Then all the notations of thirty poems in the
Bingham collection on microfilm [12] (every tenth poem in packets
80 to 91,[13] spanning the years of composition from 1858 to
1872) were thoroughly analyzed to determine the precise
method of classification for this edition.

The broader search of all the manuscripts of poetry and many
of the letters in the Harvard, Amherst, and Boston Public
Library collections distinguished seven basic marks of punctuation appearing consistently: the period, the question mark, the
exclamation point, and four "irregular" notations: ($\prime$), ($\scriptstyle\backslash$),
(-), and ($\smile$), in varying lengths, degrees of slant, and positions
in relation to the writing line. The marks resembling a dash
(-) and a comma ($\prime$) were classified as irregular because their
appearance often violated their specific grammatical use, and
because the "comma" was often placed considerably above the
writing line—after an interjection ("Ah'"), for instance. One
other mark was distinguished, a dividing vertical (|), but be-

---

[12] Folger, 168.1. Reproduced by the Library of Congress Photoduplica-
tion Service.

[13] Numbered: (Bingham 1a, 3b, and 105-2) in packet 80; (Bingham 8c
and 10c) in packet 81; (Bingham 13a and 15c) in packet 82; (Bingham
16d, 17g, and 19e) in packet 83; (Bingham 24b and 27b) in packet 84;
(Bingham 30b) in packet 85; (Bingham 34c, 35c, 36e, and 38c) in
packet 86; (Bingham 40c, 43a, and 45a) in packet 87; (Bingham 47c,
49c, 51e, and 54a) in packet 88; (Bingham 58) in packet 89; (Bingham
61b, 62h, 65b, and 67a) in packet 90; and (Bingham 69b) in packet 91.

cause it appeared only once in all the manuscripts, and then only in a work-sheet draft (Bingham 97-4), it was not classified as basic.

The closer analysis consisted of classifying each mark of punctuation in the thirty poems described above and measuring the length, and degree of slant, and the position in relation to the writing line of all the "irregular" marks. This analysis revealed the following information.

1. The 265 separate notations could be classified and counted:

periods	: 15
question marks	: 2
exclamation points	: 27
total conventional marks	: 44

angular slants (,)	: 51
reversed slants (‚)	: 66
horizontal marks (-)	: 99
curved marks (˘) (‿)	: 5

2. Of the 44 conventional marks, only one exclamation point showed any irregularity, as the lower character of the mark was a horizontal dash rather than the conventional period (!).

3. The "irregular" notations measured approximately one-sixteenth of an inch, their length varying slightly with the proportionate size of the handwriting or with its normal irregularities. Three of the horizontal notations, however, were more than twice the length of the others, and of these, one had a slight twirl (～).

4. Every conventional mark of punctuation was placed in the standard position near the base of the writing line.

5. Most of the notations classified as horizontal appeared in

the position of the conventional dash, approximately at mid-line or somewhat lower. A very few were placed as low as the writing line.

6. Of the 51 notations classified as "angular slants," 50 were placed approximately in the conventional position of the comma, rising from below to the writing line, or slightly above (ˏ) or (ˏ); one was placed definitely above the writing line (ˏ).

7. Of the 66 notations classified as "reversed slants," 53 were in the same approximate position of the comma (ˏ), but 13 were placed lower and under the last letter of the word preceding ("word").

8. Most of the 99 notations classified as horizontal had little or no slant; a very few had as much of a slant as 12° up or down, but most slants did not exceed 5°.

9. Of the five notations classified as "curved," one appeared in the position of the horizontal notation approximately at mid-line (ˬ), and four were placed on end, falling from the writing line (˻).

10. The angle of slant of the 51 angular notations varied from 23° to 55°, but most of these fell in the range of 30° to 55°.

11. The angle of slant of the 66 reversed slants varied from 15° to 75°. Of these, the great majority fell also in the 30° to 55° range. Only a few measured less than 20°, and these were classified as reversed slants because of their position decidedly below the writing line.

12. The angle of curve of the five notations classified as curved exceeded 15°. A few horizontal notations showed very slight curves (less than 10°), as, for instance, Dickinson's crossing of her "t's" is often slightly curved.

13. All the notations, conventional and "irregular," with the exception of the 13 lower reversed slants, were placed after the

words they punctuated. The slants, circumflexes, and conventional marks usually appeared immediately after the word; the horizontal mark was normally placed one letter space beyond, so that it appeared halfway between the preceding word and the word following ("word" - "word").

14. The notations in these thirty poems of the Bingham collection included all the formations and positions of Emily Dickinson's punctuation system observed in the broader search except for the third and very high position of the angular slant, as, for instance, it appears in line one of Poem 177 ("Ah´ Necromancy Sweet!"); a second formation of the question mark, which substitutes the horizontal notation for the period, as in line five of Poem 621 ("Brazil ? He twirled a Button -"); and a third formation of the exclamation point, which substitutes the angular slant for the period, as in line eight of Poem 239 ("There - Paradise - is found !").

On the basis of the findings described, the notations in this edition have been transcribed from the manuscripts as follows: All notations appearing at or above the writing line with a slant of less than 13° are marked with the horizontal dash (-); of these marks, only those more than twice as long as others in the same manuscript are transcribed as "extra-long" (—). All notations with a reversed angular slant exceeding 20° are transcribed as angular slants (,), and their appearance definitely above (⸴) or high above (´) the writing line is so indicated. All notations with a reversed angular slant exceeding 20° are transcribed as such (،). Those having a lesser degree of slant that appear definitely below the writing line are transcribed as reversed slants, but the exception to the standard rule of classification is noted below the text of the poem, along with other pertinent data about the manuscript. Reversed slants appearing low and below the last letter of the word they punctuate are transcribed in this position ("word"). All notations with curves exceeding

15° are transcribed as curved, either horizontal (⌣) or "falling" (⌓). Those notations with slight curves only (less than 15°) are transcribed according to their straight-line classification, but the possibility of another classification is noted below the poem. With the exception of the low reversed slant, all notations are placed after the words they punctuate to correspond to the standard spacing of the manuscripts. The conventional marks, the two angular slants and the curved marks are placed immediately after the word; the horizontal mark, one letter space beyond. Any variance from the standard spacing is noted below the poem.

Nineteenth-Century Elocution

The explanation of the four elocutionary symbols which correspond exactly in form to the four basic marks of punctuation in the Dickinson manuscripts can be found in almost any nineteenth-century elocution text, and where other elocutionary symbols and principles may vary somewhat with the individual text, there seem to be no significant differences among the elocutionists in their use of the inflectional symbols or in their explanations of the principles of inflection. Ebenezer Porter, however, is the most likely source of Dickinson's elocutionary knowledge since it is his *Rhetorical Reader* that is listed as the standard text for the elocution classes in the Amherst Academy catalogues for 1840–1847, the years of the poet's registered attendance there. Because Emily Dickinson must have been well acquainted with this text, both in the classroom and during the Wednesday afternoon rhetorical exercises (which she refers to several times in her early letters, and for which Frederick Tuckerman says it was one of the standard texts),[14] the *Rhe-*

---

[14] Frederick Tuckerman, *Amherst Academy* (Amherst: Printed for the Trustees, 1929), p. 100; hereafter cited as *Amherst Academy*. I am greatly indebted to Mr. Charles R. Greene, Librarian Emeritus of the Jones

torical Reader seems indispensable to any complete study of this poet's work, and even, perhaps, explains the direction of some of her thinking. For the *Reader* provides not only the technical background for understanding her particular kind of punctuation, but explains as well what seems to be much of the reasoning behind her adoption of this system.

The art of elocution is held in comparatively low esteem today, for it is connected in the minds of many with the sometimes painful recitations of children in the primary grades; thus it is indeed understandable that many a twentieth-century reader is puzzled and even dismayed to think that a poet of such stature and depth as Emily Dickinson would stoop to what now may seem a highly contrived and poetically immature technique. Considered in the context of her own time, however, Emily Dickinson's choice of punctuation can be understood in a far more sympathetic light.

In the early and middle nineteenth century, elocution was regarded as an art of a high order, and its considerable value as entertainment undoubtedly stemmed not only from its serious study as an art form but also from its inherent appeal to the great cult of sentiment which flourished then and manifested itself so strongly in the thinking and emotional attitudes of Emily Dickinson's contemporaries. Richard Chase has defined this particular cult of the time as a "watered-down version of two cultural phenomena: New England Puritanism and Romanticism," and he declares that it is not at all surprising that

Library in Amherst, for sending me a copy of this book and also for his help in checking the catalogues for me.

It should also be mentioned here that Jack L. Capps, in his recent book, *Emily Dickinson's Reading: 1836–1886* (Cambridge, Mass.: Harvard University Press, 1966), does not mention the Porter text as part of the poet's reading background. He says that "there is no record of the books she used in her early years at Amherst Academy" (p. 103). A valuable record exists both in the Amherst Academy Catalogues for 1840–1847 and in *Amherst Academy*.

Emily Dickinson "should have found sustenance in this popular sentiment, since she herself was a product, even in her best poetic moments, of the same cultural influences." Mr. Chase finds the "fine flower" of expression of the cult of sentiment in "Ik Marvell's" *Reveries of a Bachelor,* where, on every count, natural and spontaneous feelings take precedence over any "contrived" aesthetics.[15] But antecedent to the *Reveries* was Porter's *Rhetorical Reader,* where sentiment, or "true" feeling, is the key note, and the tones of natural or colloquial language become the soul of artistic expression. The term "expression" Porter defines as "the proper influences of reverential and pathetic sentiment on the voice," and he continues his explanation:

There is a modification of voice, which accompanies awakened sensibility of soul, that is more easily felt than described; and this constitutes the *unction* of delivery. Without this, thoughts that should impress, attract, or soothe the mind, often become repulsive. The fact cannot have escaped common observation, that sorrow, and its kindred passions, when carried to a high pitch, suspend the voice entirely. In a lower degree, they give it a slender and tremulous utterance. . . . The highest passion of this sort, is expressed by *silence;* and when so far moderated, as to admit of words, it speaks only in abrupt fragments of sentences. Hence it is, that all artificial *imitation,* in this case, is commonly so unlike the reality. It leads to metaphors, to amplification and embellishment, in language, and to either vociferation or whining in utterance. Whereas the real passion intended to be imitated, if it speaks at all, speaks without ornament, in few words, and in tones that

[15] Richard Chase, *Emily Dickinson* (New York: Dell Publishing Co., Inc., 1965), p. 41.

are a perfect contrast to those of declamation. The distinction arises from those laws of the human mind, by which internal emotion is connected with its external signs.

Not only does such a passage help to explain the correspondence between Emily Dickinson's "abrupt fragmentation" and the intense emotional content of much of her verse, but, as it distinguishes between "artificial" and "unornamented" "imitation" of "real passion" conveyed through the quality of the voice, it also provides a substantial reason for Emily Dickinson's choice of oral punctuation as a means of specifying or controlling tone. The poet herself makes the same distinction as Porter in a letter dated October 1869 to Perez Cowan (the same letter that speaks of dying as "a wild Night and a New Road"), in which she attempts to console the minister upon the recent loss of his sister; but finding this difficult, she says toward the end that she must put the subject "down" because "it hurts you," and concludes, "We bruise each other less in talking than in writing, for then a quiet accent helps words themselves too hard." [16] Late in her career, in August 1885, the poet drafted a letter, possibly to Sara Colton, which reads: "What a Hazard an Accent is! When I think of the Hearts it has scuttled or sunk, I almost fear to lift my Hand to so much as a punctuation-".[17] The actual letter sent contains a most interesting word change at the end: "What a hazard an Accent is! When I think of the Hearts it has scuttled or sunk, I hardly dare to raise my voice to so much as a Salutation. [signed] E. Dickinson." [18]

Further evidence of the possible reasoning behind Emily Dickinson's choice of oral punctuation can be seen in Porter's distinction between what he calls "grammatical reading" and "rhetorical reading":

[16] *Letters,* II, 463.
[17] *Ibid.,* III, 887.
[18] *Ibid.*

Grammatical reading . . . respects merely the sense of what is read. When performed audibly, for the benefit of others, it is still only the same sort of process which one performs silently, for his own benefit, when he casts his eye along the page, to ascertain the meaning of its author. The chief purpose of the correct reader is to be intelligible; and this requires an accurate perception of grammatical relation in the structure of sentences; a due regard to accent and pauses, to strength of voice, and clearness of utterance.

Rhetorical reading has a higher object, and calls into action higher powers. It is not applicable to a composition destitute of emotion, for it supposes *feeling*. It does not barely express the thoughts of an author, but expresses them with the force, variety, and beauty, which feeling demands. (p. 21)

Closely allied to the intonational patterns of speech to convey "feeling" is the use of natural or colloquial language (as opposed to "artificial"). Another passage in the *Rhetorical Reader* explains Porter's selection of examples to illustrate the rhetorical principles as they are presented. The reasoning seems to correspond significantly to Emily Dickinson's choice of oral punctuation and the colloquial tongue.

In order to render the new classifications which I have given intelligible, I have chosen examples chiefly from colloquial language; because the tones of conversation ought to be the basis of delivery, and because these only are at once recognized by the ear. Being conformed to nature, they are instinctively right; so that scarcely a man in a million uses artificial tones in conversation. And this one fact, I remark in passing, furnishes a standing canon to the learner in elocution. In contending with any bad habit of

> voice, let him break up the sentence on which the difficulty occurs, and throw it, if possible, into the colloquial form. Let him observe in himself and others, the turns of voice which occur in speaking, familiarly and earnestly, on common occasions. (p. 28)

The two major principles discussed in the *Rhetorical Reader* are called "inflection" and "emphasis." Both principles, plus a third, referred to as "rhetorical pause," are incorporated into Emily Dickinson's oral punctuation. Chapter III explains what is meant by "inflection." It begins:

> The absolute modifications of the voice in speaking are four; namely, monotone, rising inflection, falling inflection, and circumflex. The first may be marked to the eye by a horizontal line, thus, (-) the second thus, (ˊ) the third thus, (ˋ) the fourth thus (˘).
>
> The monotone is a sameness of sound on successive syllables, which resembles that produced by repeated strokes on a bell. Unseemly as this is, where varied inflections are required, it more or less belongs to grave delivery, especially in elevated description, or where emotions of sublimity or reverence are expressed; as,—
>
> He rōde upon ā chērūb and dīd flȳ.—I sāw a grēat whīte thrōne, and hīm that sāt on it.
>
> The rising inflection turns the voice upward, or ends higher than it begins. It is heard invariably in the direct question; as, *Will you go todáy?*
>
> The falling inflection turns the voice downwards, or ends lower than it begins. It is heard in the answer to a question; as, *Nò; I shall go tomòrrow.*
>
> The circumflex is a union of the two inflections, sometimes on one syllable, and sometimes on several. It begins

with the falling, and ends with the rising slide; as, *I may go to-mŏrrow, though I cannot go todày.* (pp. 27–28)

Twelve rules of inflection are then explained in detail (pp. 29–38); their essential points, along with some notes and illustrations, follow:

Rule I. When the disjunctive *or* connects words or clauses, it has the rising inflection before, and the falling after it. . . .

Rule II. The direct question, or that which admits the answer of *yes* or *no,* has the rising inflection, and the answer has the falling. . . .

Note. When exclamation becomes a question, it demands the rising slide; as, "How, you say, are we to accòmplish it? How accómplish it! Certainly not by fearing to attempt it."

Rule III. When *negation* is opposed to *affirmation* the former has the rising, and the latter the falling inflection. . . .

Note. Negation alone, not opposed to affirmation, generally inclines the voice to the rising slide, but not *always,* as some respectable teachers have maintained. "Thou shalt not kìll;" "Thou shalt not stèal;"—are negative precepts, in which the falling slide must be used; and the simple particle *no,* with the intensive falling slide, is one of the strongest monosyllables in the language.

Rule IV. The *pause* of *suspension,* denoting that the sense is unfinished, requires the rising inflection. . . .

This rule embraces several particulars, more especially applying to sentences of the periodic structure, which consist of several members, but form no complete sense before the close. It is a first principle of articulate language, that in such a case, the voice should be kept suspended, to denote continuation of sense.

Rule V. Tender emotion generally inclines the voice to the rising slide. . . .

Grief, compassion, and delicate affection, soften the soul, and are uttered in words, invariably with corresponding qualities of voice.

Hence the *vocative* case, when it expresses either affection or delicate respect, takes the rising slide. . . .

The same slide prevails in pathetic poetry.

> Thus with the year,
> Seasons retùrn; but not to me returns,
> Dáy, or the sweet approach of év'n or mórn,
> Or sight of vernal blóom, or summer's róse,
> Or flócks, or hérds, or human face divíne;
> But clòud instead, and ever during dàrk
> Surround me

Rule VI. The rising slide is commonly used at the last pause but one in a sentence. The reason is, that the ear expects the voice to fall when the sense is finished; and therefore it should rise for the sake of variety and harmony, on the pause that precedes the cadence. . . .

Rule VII. The *indirect question*, or that which is not answered by *yes* or *no*, has the falling inflection; and its *answer* has the same. . . .

Rule VIII. The language of *authority*, of *surprise*, and of *distress*, is commonly uttered with the falling inflection. . . .

Rule IX. Emphatic *succession* of particulars requires the falling slide. The reason is, that a distinctive utterance is necessary to fix the attention of each particular. . . .

The rising slide . . . as it occurs in an emphatic series of direct questions, rises higher on each particular, as it proceeds.

Rule X. Emphatic *repetition* requires the falling slide. . . .

Rule XI. The final pause requires the falling slide. . . .

Rule XII. The circumflex occurs chiefly where the language is either *hypothetical* or *ironical*. The most common use of it is to express, indefinitely or conditionally, some idea that is contrasted with another idea, expressed or understood, to which the falling slide belongs; thus:—*Hume said he would go twenty miles, to hear Whĭtefield preach.* The contrast suggested by the circumflex here is,—*though he would take no pains to hear a còmmon preacher.*

You ask a physician concerning your friend who is dangerously sick, and receive this reply,—*he is bĕtter.* The circumflex denotes only a partial, doubtful amendment, and implies—*But he is still dangerously sick.* . . .

This circumflex when indistinct, coincides nearly with the rising slide; when distinct, it denotes qualified affirmation instead of that which is positive, as marked by the falling slide. . . .

In a later section, Porter also discusses the close resemblance between the rising slide and the circumflex, and makes a further distinction between these and the falling slide. He illustrates his point by first giving examples of the three uses of the circumflex:

Ironically;
They tell us to be moderate; but *thĕy, thĕy* are to revel in profusion.

Hypothetically;
If men see our faults, they talk among *thĕmselves* though
we refuse to let them talk to *ùs.*

Comparatively;

> The beggar was *blìnd* as well as *lăme.*
> He is more *knàve* than *foŏl.*

In such a connexion of two correlate words, whether in
contrast or comparison, the most *prominent* of the two in
sense, that in which the essence of the thought lies, commonly has the strong, falling emphasis; and that which
expresses something subordinate or circumstantial, has the
rising. The same rising or circumflex emphasis prevails where
the thought is *conditional,* or something is *implied* or *insinuated,* rather than strongly expressed.

The amount is, that generally the weaker emphasis, where
there is tender, or conditional, or partial enunciation of
thought, requires the voice to *rise:* while the strong emphasis, where the thought is bold, and the language positive, adopts the falling slide, except where some counter-
acting principle occurs, as in the interrogative inflection.

In still another section devoted to the proper reading of poetry, the first three of six general rules (pp. 64–66) relate to
inflectional principles:

1. In proportion as the sentiment of a passage is elevated, inspiring emotions of dignity or reverence, the voice
has less variety of inflection, and is more inclined to the
monotone.
2. When the sentiment of a passage is delicate and gentle, especially when it is plaintive, it inclines the voice to

the rising inflection; and for this reason, poetry oftener requires the rising inflection than prose: yet,

3. The *rights of emphasis* must be respected in poetry.
When the language of a passage is strong and discriminating, or familiarly descriptive, or colloquial,—the same
modifications of voice are required as in prose. The *emphatic stress* and *inflection,* that must be *intensive,* in prose,
to express a thought forcibly, are equally necessary in poetry. . . .

Emily Dickinson's Rhetorical Punctuation

Inflection

In nineteenth-century elocution, then, we can find a full explanation of the intonational function of the four "irregular"
notations of Dickinson's punctuation system. It should be
noted, however, that Porter places the inflectional symbols over
the stressed vowels of the words and retains the marks of conventional punctuation in the line itself—a common practice
among the elocutionists, who were using these symbols for
directional purposes only. Dickinson's major innovation is to
substitute the rhetorical symbols for conventional punctuation
(retaining only the period, question mark, and exclamation
point for their inherent rhetorical value), consistently plac-
ing them between words in the position of conventional punctuation. In her line, then, the inflectional notations will register
first of all the corresponding slide or turn heard with the word
immediately preceding.

According to Porter, the rising slide indicates a number of
tonal qualities: (1) the subordinate, conditional, or negative
terms of a comparison, implied or directly stated; (2) negation
alone; (3) the direct question; (4) suspension of thought, denoting incompleteness or continuation of sense; (5) tender emo-

tion, such as grief, compassion, and delicate affection; and (6) closely allied to the circumflex, something implied or insinuated. The qualities listed in items one, four, and six all seem to apply in some degree to the tone and meaning behind the lines of Poem 510, where the rising slide predominates throughout the first four stanzas, all of which describe a particular experience (in progressively more precise imagery) in terms of what it was *not*, only what it was *like*:

It was not Death, for I stood up,
And all the Dead, lie down -
It was not Night, for all the Bells
Put out their Tongues, for Noon.

It was not Frost, for on my Flesh
I felt Siroccos - crawl -
Nor Fire - for just my Marble feet
Could keep a Chancel ⸲ cool -

And yet, it tasted, like them all ⸲
The Figures I have seen
Set orderly, for Burial ⸲
Reminded me, of mine -

As if my life were shaven,
And fitted to a frame,
And could not breathe without a key,
And 'twas like Midnight, some -

When everything that ticked ⸲ has stopped -
And Space stares ⸲ all around -
Or Grisly frosts ⸲ first Autumn morns,
Repeal the Beating Ground -

> But , most , like Chaos - Stopless - cool -
> Without a Chance , or Spar -
> Or even a Report of Land ,
> To justify - Despair.

Here the rising slides (the two positions of which will be discussed later) seem to indicate not only suspension of thought and the negative terms of a comparison ("it was not this, but something else"), but an implication of something extremely meaningful beyond that which is actually described—the indescribable essence of the real experience. The two concluding stanzas come closest to this reality, as the predominant tone shifts to the more forcible falling inflection and the grave monotone.

In Poem 810 the rising slide also predominates. But here the subject matter alone seems to indicate a tone of gentleness and delicate affection, although a possible undercurrent of irony is not ruled out:

> Her Grace is all she has ,
> And that , so least displays ,
> One Art , to recognize , must be ,
> Another Art , to praise

The falling slide conveys the least ambiguous tone of all the notations. It denotes emphatic force, authority, conclusiveness, decided affirmation, surprise, distress, disgust. Thus a forcible tone of angry disgust or distress is immediately registered by the falling slide in the opening line of Poem 861:

> Split the Lark   and you'll find the Music -

The circumflex expresses a stronger conditional, hypothetical, or ironical tone than the rising slide, although, as Porter says, it is closely allied in intonational quality and meaning. The circumflex is the least frequent notation in Dickinson's line, but it can be effective in the decided irony that its "twist" registers. For example, the special emphasis afforded "stares" in line 18 of "It was not Death, " calls attention to the paradox of space staring back. Similarly, in line 15 of "Because I could not stop for Death -" (Poem 712), the circumflex after "Gown," the only such notation in the whole poem, points to the paradoxical nature of the funeral-bridal attire:

> For Only Gossamer ⸱ My Gown ˘

Porter does not have a specific notation which resembles Dickinson's "falling" circumflex, but William McGuffey's popular *Sixth Eclectic Reader* (now available in a Signet Classic paperback edition, published by The New American Library, 1963 [a reprint of the 1879 edition]) includes a fifth inflectional notation called the "falling circumflex" (ʌ), which registers a combination of the rising and falling inflections on the same sound, the reverse of the regular circumflex. This seems to be almost the same intonational effect Porter recognizes in a note to Rule III in his list of inflectional principles, where he ex plains that in order to distinguish clearly between the rising and the falling slides in opposition, the latter should be "protracted" from "a high note to a low one," and not struck as usual by merely "dropping to a low note" from the normal speaking key. Since Porter also indicates the close resemblance of the normal circumflex to the rising slide, it would seem that this "protracted" falling slide is much the same as McGuffey's "falling circumflex" and is the particular effect that Dickinson is registering with her symbol of the circumflex on end (˘).

The most frequent notation in Dickinson's line is the symbol for the monotone, which holds the voice to a "sameness of sound on successive syllables" and suggests a tone of grave seri-

ousness, elevated emotion, deliberateness, dignity, awe, reverence, and the like. The predominant monotone of Dickinson's
work thus registers a tone principally *devoid* of the varied inflections of normal conversational speech and conveys a note
of grave seriousness to lines that might possibly be read otherwise. For example, there is nothing in the least gay or effusive
in the tone of the opening lines of Poem 754:

> My Life had stood - a Loaded Gun -
> In Corners - till a Day
> The Owner passed - identified -
> And carried Me away -

As evident in the examples given above, most of Dickinson's
notations are placed in the standard position of conventional
punctuation; but sometimes, as in lines eight, nine, and eleven
of "It was not Death , ", a rising slide will appear noticeably
above the writing line (and sometimes very high above) and a
falling slide noticeably lower and under the last letter of the
word it punctuates. These distinctions seem to be adequately
explained by Porter when he distinguishes between what he
calls the "common" and the "intensive" rising and falling slides
(p. 27):

> As the whole doctrine of inflections depends on these two
> simple slides of the voice, one more explanation seems nec-
> essary, as to the degree in which each is applied, under
> different circumstances. In most cases where the rising slide
> is used, it is only a gentle turn of the voice upward, one or
> two notes. In cases of emotion, as in the spirited, direct
> question, the slide may pass through five or eight notes.
> The former may be called the *common* rising inflection, the

latter the *intensive*. Just the same distinction exists in the falling inflection. In the question, uttered with surprise, "Are you going todáy?" the slide is intensive. But in the following case, it is common, "as fame is but breàth, as riches are trànsitory, and life itself is uncértain, so we should seek a better portion."

In Dickinson's line a more decided emphasis upon the word is given with the intensive, or higher or lower, slides (or, for that matter, with the even more intensive circumflexes). With the rising slide, the degree of intensity, or the number of notes to be heard in the slide, will correspond to the height of the slide, as it will appear either in the second position just above the writing line, or in the third position, very high above the line. The second position would register approximately a five-note slide upward; the third, the full-pitch scale. The third or highest position of the rising slide, as it appears, for instance, in the first line of Poem 177 ("Ah ´ Necromancy Sweet!") corresponds to the highest pitch of the voice recognized by contemporary linguists who have established, as basic, four pitches to the speaking voice: the first, "low"; the second, "normal"; the third, "high"; the fourth, "very high." Dickinson's system does not seem to register a "very low" slide to correspond to "very high," but Porter indirectly recognizes the impossibility of reaching such a low pitch when he suggests that an effective falling slide should sometimes be begun high. Neither, of course, do the linguists recognize a "very low" pitch.

The second position of the rising slide, then, registers a lesser degree of intensity than the third, but is more emphatic than the first or "common" position. Similarly, the lower position of the falling slide makes the same distinction in emphasis from the common or standard position.

Rhetorical Pause

As Dickinson's punctuation registers the meaningful intonations
to be heard in her line, its purpose seems to be somewhat like
the attempts of the modern linguists to establish a closer relation between the spoken and the written language. In his
chapter on punctuation, Harold Whitehall asserts that the traditional purpose of punctuation is "to symbolize by means of
visual signs the patterns heard in speech." [19] A more succinct
definition of the purpose of Emily Dickinson's punctuation
would be hard to find. But the linguists have not as yet gone
much beyond a descriptive analysis of the spoken language in
their attempts to reorient conventional grammatical principles
in terms more closely and more precisely related to English
speech patterns—especially in the area of punctuation. They
have not as yet, like Dickinson, devised any new system of
punctuation, and their phonemic symbology is like that of the
elocutionists, superimposed ("suprasegmental") upon the written line. Nevertheless, certain striking similarities between
Emily Dickinson's thinking and that of the linguists invite discussion.

The linguists, for example, do not deal specifically with the
elocutionary principle of inflection, but the phonemic quality
of a "clause terminal" is much the same thing. In *An Introduction to Descriptive Linguistics,* H. A. Gleason describes this
particular feature as follows:

> Clause terminals are popularly referred to as "pauses."
> There may be an actual pause, but this is not necessary.
> If there is a pause, it is always preceded by one of the char-

---

[19] Harold Whitehall, *Structural Essentials of English.* (New York: Harcourt, Brace and World, Inc., 1956), p. 119; hereafter cited as *Structural
Essentials of English.*

acteristic English clause terminals. The clause terminal is, properly speaking, a means of ending a clause, not of separating two clauses, and for this reason one such terminal will be found at the end of the last clause in an utterance.

Clause terminals are of three kinds:

[↘] fading: a rapid trailing away of the voice into silence. Both the pitch and volume decrease rapidly.

[↗] rising: a sudden, rapid, but short rise in the pitch. The volume does not trail off so noticeably, but seems to be comparatively sharply cut off.

[→] sustained: a sustention of the pitch accompanied by prolongation of the last syllable of the clause and some diminishing of volume.[20]

Before the linguists, Dickinson recognized that the two features of inflection and pause were combined, because in her line the inflectional notation registers both these qualities of a "clause terminal" at once. Porter's placement of the inflectional notations above the words indicates that he does not make this particular distinction; but "rhetorical pause" is still an important concern of the elocutionists. Alexander M. Bell, another noted elocutionist of Dickinson's time, has this to say in the Introduction to his *Principles of Elocution* about the importance of pause and the inadequacy of conventional punctuation to register it properly:

The marks of punctuation are taught in schools as measures of the pauses in reading. Children are told to stop at all the "stops," and only at the stops, and to proportion their stopping to the supposed time-value of the stops. But

[20] H. A. Gleason, *An Introduction to Descriptive Linguistics* (New York: Holt, Rinehart and Winston, 1961), p. 46.

the marks of punctuation have no relation to time; nor are they at all intended to regulate the pauses of a reader. They have a purpose, but it is not this. They do, in the majority of cases, occur where pauses should be made, but they do not supply nearly the number of pauses that good reading requires. They simply mark the grammatical construction of a sentence. While word follows word in strict grammatical relation, no comma is inserted, though many pauses may be indispensable; and wherever any break occurs in the grammatical relation of proximate words, there a comma is written, though, often, a pause would spoil the sense. Commas are placed before and after all interpolations that separate related words—adjective and noun, adverb and adjective, pronoun and verb, verb and object, etc.;—but they are not written while words follow each other *in direct and mutual relation*. Punctuation has thus no reference to delivery; it has no claim to regulate reading; and nothing but ignorance of a better guide could have led to the adoption of the grammatical points to direct the voice in pausing.[21]

Porter follows much the same line of thinking when he refers to "visible" punctuation as an imperfect guide to "quantity" as well as inflection:

Often the voice must rest, where no pause is allowed in grammar; especially does this happen, when the speaker would fix attention on a single word, that stands as immediate nominative to a verb. As

Prosperity gains friends, *adversity* tries them.
Some place the bliss in action, *some* in ease;
Those call it pleasure, and contentment these.

[21] Alexander M. Bell, *Principles of Elocution* (Salem, Mass: J. P. Burbank, 1878), pp. xxii–iii.

Here the words in Italic take visible pause after them, without violence to grammatical relation. But the *ear* demands a pause after each of these words, which no good reader will fail to observe.

The same principle extends to the *length* of pauses. The comma, when it simply marks grammatical relation, is very short, as "He took with him Peter, and James, and John, his disciples." But when the comma is used in language of emotion, though it is the same pause to the eye, it may suspend the voice much longer than in the former case; as in the solemn and deliberate call to attention;—"Men, brethren, and fathers, hearken." (p. 57)

The nineteenth-century elocutionists, then, like the contemporary linguists, did not believe (as did the eighteenth-century grammarians) that grammatical pause bears a specific relation to time. As Harold Whitehall has said, pause is "simply pause," [22] and asserts, with Bell and Porter, that it has little relation to time and less to the marks of conventional punctuation. Nevertheless, both the linguists and the elocutionists recognize a distinction between an ordinary vocal pause and what Porter refers to further as an "emphatic pause"—made before or after a "striking thought" or word (p. 57)—or what the linguists have termed a "metalinguistic" or "overlength" pause.[23] Dickinson's conspicuously long dash may well represent this same emphatic or metalinguistic pause, distinguishing it, for purposes of special emphasis, from the regular vocal pause which her notations automatically register along with the inflections.[24]

[22] *Structural Essentials of English*, p. 118.

[23] As referred to specifically in a footnote to the essay presenting a phonemic analysis of Robert Frost's "Mowing," by Seymour Chatman in *Kenyon Review*, XVIII (1956), 431.

[24] Although, as already shown, Dickinson's notations approximate for the most part the length of a standard grammatical dash, sometimes, even in the same manuscript, the notations may vary enough in size to war-

But of seemingly more importance than the specific length of the pause indicated is the function of the notations, as supplements to conventional punctuation, to register the meaningful pauses themselves, and thus to act as an explicit timing device which provides its own particular emphasis, helping to define the degree of emotional intensity behind the poem. In the section on "quantity" Porter says:

> But *time* in elocution, has a larger application than that which respects words and clauses, I mean that which respects the general *rate* of delivery. In this case, it is not practicable, as in music, nor perhaps desirable, to establish a fixed standard, to which every reader or speaker shall conform. The habits of different men may differ considerably in rate of utterance, without being chargeable with fault. But I refer rather to the difference which emotion will produce, in the rate of the same individual. I have said before, that those passions which quicken or retard a man's step in walking, will produce a similar effect on his voice in speaking. Narration is equable and flowing; vehemence, firm and accelerated; anger and joy, rapid. Whereas dignity, authority, sublimity, awe,—assume deeper tones, and a slower movement. Accordingly we sometimes hear a good reader or speaker, when there is some sudden turn of thought, check

rant a possible classification of as many as four or five different lengths— to include, for instance, an "extra-short" dash. The classification in this edition, however, has been restricted to "regular" and "emphatic," or overlength, because (1) there appears to be no sound basis in the actual patterns of speech (where Dickinson's fine ear could distinguish, ahead of the linguists, the combined features of a clause terminal) to warrant distinctions in pause lengths beyond regular and emphatic, and (2) because there seems to be no consistency in the appearance of a very short dash; one may, for instance, appear at the very end of a stanza or poem as well as within the line, where it might make more sense, and (3) because the very natural and inherent irregularities of handwriting explain minor discrepancies such as slight curves to lines meant to be straight and slight variations in standard length.

himself in the full current of utterance, and give indescribable power to a sentence, or part of a sentence, by dropping his voice, and adopting a slow, full pronunciation. (p. 56)

The predominant tone registered by the notations of the Dickinson manuscripts is the monotone, expressing, as it does, emotional qualities appropriate to most of the poetry's ultimate high seriousness; but, as Mrs. Ward has said, the frequency of the notations may vary considerably from poem to poem (or from letter to letter) and seems to bear a definite relation to the emotional intensity of the writing. Thus, although the monotone notation predominates in two such poems as "Title divine, is mine." (Poem 1072) and the description of the snowstorm, beginning "It sifts from Leaden Sieves" (Poem 311), the first poem contains far more notations (especially "interrupting" notations) than the second. But the first is rendered in highly compressed phrasing, set off by the notations, and its subject matter expresses a heightened emotional state which corresponds directly with the slow, checked pace indicated by the many pauses (or "junctures," as the linguists would say). The second poem, in contrast, is far less compressed and restrained, more emotionally detached, more flowing, hence, contains fewer "breaking" notations.

Another of Porter's six principles devoted specifically to the reading of poetry is concerned with pause:

The *pauses* of verse should be so managed, if possible, as most fully to exhibit the sense, without sacrificing the harmony of the composition. No good reader can fail to observe the *caesural* pause, occurring after the fourth syllable, in these flowing lines:

Warms in the sun ‖ refreshes in the breeze,
Glows in the stars ‖ and blossoms in the trees.

Yet no good reader would introduce the same pause from regard to melody, where the sense utterly forbids it, as in this line;

I sit, with sad ‖ civility I read.

There is another poetical pause, occurring at the *end of the line*. In blank verse, even when the sense of one line runs closely into the next, the reader may *generally*, not always, mark the end of the line, by a proper protraction and suspension of voice, on the closing syllable.

Because the notations in Dickinson's line function grammatically as well as rhetorically, the pauses, or junctures, they register occur where sense as well as timing demands; and when Porter refers to the "poetical pause, occurring at the *end of the line*," which the reader may "generally, not always, mark . . . by a proper protraction and suspension of voice, on the closing syllable," he is touching upon a principle that must have been of special concern to Emily Dickinson when we consider her complaint to T. W. Higginson of the editorial insertion of a comma in one of her published poems (986). The comma had "defeated" the poem of the third line, she said, when "the third and fourth were one." [25] Thus the "stop" syntactical function of Dickinson's notations should not be taken lightly—especially when the lack of a notation at a line's end indicates that the line is run on. Sometimes, however, the lack of terminal punctuation—either for a line, a stanza, or a whole poem—seems to suggest a purposeful "nonconclusion" or ambiguity. For instance, the absence of any concluding notations in both stanzas of "This is My letter to the World" (Poem 441) indicates the possibility of a kind of open-endedness to the thought—the hint of a question (or an intentional ambiguity at the close of the

[25] *Letters*, II, 450.

first stanza and the opening of the second: did "Nature" tell the news "with tender Majesty," or is it being committed by the poet with such—or possibly both?).

The most frequent concluding notation in Dickinson's poetry is the symbol for the monotone, which registers a similar but less pointed inconclusiveness. The grammatical period, with its definite note of finality appears seldom, indicating, it would seem, the poet's reluctance to make final pronouncements. But the period can at times convey a heightened meaning of its own, especially if it appears as other than a concluding notation. For example, the period at the end of the first line of "I know that He exists." (Poem 338) conveys a sense of dogmatic assurance to the opening statement appropriate both to the traditional Christian belief in the existence of a benevolent God and to the optimistic "sight" of the American Transcendentalists. But as the opening optimism is almost completely undermined in the rest of the poem, the concluding exclamation point registers a decidedly contrasting note of emphatic distress in keeping with the conjecture here expressed of the concept of a distinctly malevolent "other force."

The emphatic stress of an exclamation is normally registered by a falling slide, but sometimes Dickinson's exclamation point may be combined with the rising slide or the monotone dash, rather than the conventional period, to indicate that the exclamatory word is heard either with a slide or on a sustained level of pitch. Poem 239 shows all three versions of the exclamation point as the terminal point for each of the three stanzas, in an order (!), (!), and (!) which establishes a kind of emphatic succession of its own. The question mark is sometimes similarly modified in the Dickinson manuscripts. The modifications of both these conventional points to register a precise inflection seem to be based on Porter's thinking, when he says:

Rhetorical punctuation has a few marks of its own, as the point of interrogation, and of admiration, the parenthesis, and the hyphen, all of which denote no grammatical relation, and have no established length. And there is no good reason, if such marks are used at all, why they should not be rendered more adequate to their purpose.

The interrogative mark, for example, is used to denote, not length of pause, but appropriate modification of voice, at the end of a question. But it happens that this one mark as now used represents two things, that are exactly contrary to each other. When the child is taught, as he still is in many schools, always to raise his voice in finishing a question, he finds it easy to do so in a case like this,—"Will you go todáy?"—"Are they Hébrews?" But when he comes to the *indirect* question, not answered by *yes*, or *no*, his instinct, as I have said before, rebels against the rule, and he spontaneously reads with the falling slide, *"Why are you silent? Why do you prevàricate?"* Now, in this latter case, if the usual mark of interrogation were inverted, (¿) when its office is to turn the voice downward, it would be discriminating, and significant of its design. (p. 57)

Emphasis

Chapter V of the *Rhetorical Reader* takes up a third and most important rhetorical principle—that of emphasis, which, in most respects, includes and yet transcends all the other principles. This chapter's opening paragraph stresses the reason for this importance:

Emphasis is governed by the laws of sentiment, being inseparably associated with thought and emotion. It is the most important principle, by which elocution is related to the operations of mind. Hence when it stands opposed to the claims of custom or of harmony, these always give way to its supremacy. (p. 39)

Emphasis is defined as "a distinctive utterance of words, which are especially significant, with such a degree and kind of stress, as conveys their meaning in the best manner (p. 39)." In distinguishing between "emphatic stress" and "emphatic inflection," Porter devotes the first section of this chapter to the former, which "consists chiefly in the *loudness* of the note, but includes also the time in which important words are uttered." A good reader or speaker, he says, "when he utters a word on which the meaning of a sentence is suspended, spontaneously dwells on that word, according to the intensity of its meaning." In other words, whenever a word becomes important in sense, "it demands a correspondent stress of voice." To illustrate his point, Porter underscores the stressed word in several examples. For instance,

"Then said the high priest, are these things só?"
And then he adds:

These illustrations show that the principle of emphatic stress is perfectly simple; and that it falls on a particular word, not chiefly because that word belongs to one or another class in grammar, but because, in the present case, it is important in *sense*. To designate the words that are thus important, by the action of the voice in emphasis, is just what the etymological import of this term implies, namely, to show, to point out, to make manifest. (p. 40)

In the second section on "Emphatic Inflection," Porter distinguishes between *degree* of stress, as explained by emphatic stress, and *kind* of stress, which incorporates the principle of inflection:

> The *kind* of stress is not less important to the sense, than the degree. . . . Strong emphasis demands, in all cases, an appropriate inflection; and . . . to change this inflection perverts the sense.
>
> > The fault, dear Brutus, is not in our *stárs*;
> > But in *oursèlves*, that we are underlings;
>
> The rising inflection or circumflex on *stars* and the falling inflection on *ourselves* is so indispensable, that no reader of the least taste would mistake the one for the other. (p. 43)

Again, the stressed words are italicized in the examples, but in the reading exercises appended to the explanatory sections of the *Rhetorical Reader*, comprising about two-thirds of the book (mostly long excerpts from the Bible, Shakespeare, and several of the major seventeenth- and eighteenth-century British poets, especially Milton and Pope—the reading material for the Wednesday afternoon rhetorical exercises), Porter explains in an introductory note how the exercises should be read according to the principles and examples already studied:

> Under the several heads, a *rhetorical notation*, according to the Key given at the beginning, is so applied as to designate *inflection*, *emphasis*, and towards the close, *modulation*. When emphatic stress is but moderate, it is often distinguished only by the mark of inflection; when the stress amounts to decided emphasis, it is denoted by the Italic type; and sometimes, when strongly intensive, by

small capitals. In examples taken from the Scriptures, Italic words are used, not as in the English Bible, but solely to express *emphasis*. (p. 100) [26]

Emily Dickinson's punctuation can be interpreted to register much the same discrimination in emphasis that Porter's capitals, italics and inflectional notations indicate, and in much the same order. Although Dickinson will on occasion underscore a stressed word ("A *wounded* Deer , leaps highest ," [Poem 165]),her consistent means of indicating the most emphatic word is by the capital letter. The capitalized word will register primary stress, whether or not it is followed by an inflectional notation (for sometimes a pause will not be called for after the significant word); the inflected word, uncapitalized, will register a lesser degree of stress—perhaps "secondary" in terms of phonemic scansion; and the uncapitalized, uninflected word, which is automatically stressed by the logical base, will register the next weaker, or "tertiary," stress. Even finer degrees of emphasis will be registered by the inflectional notation itself, depending on whether it is "common" or "intensive" (or on the degree of its intensity), or a circumflex, and by the infrequently underscored word—as in the example, where "*wounded*" registers a stronger

---

[26] The Key referred to reads:

Key of Rhetorical Notation

Key of Inflection
- denotes monotone.
, rising inflection.
, falling inflection.
⌣circumflex.

Key of Modulation

(0) high.	(··) slow.
(00) high and loud.	(=) quick.
(0) low.	(−) plaintive.
(00) low and loud.	(‖) rhetorical pause
	(<) increase.

stress than normally called for by the logical base—about as
strong as if it were inflected, but not as strong as if it were
capitalized.

The variety of emphasis that Dickinson's punctuation affords
successfully counterbalances both the potential rigidity of her
hymnal meters (in keeping with another of Porter's rules for
poetry reading that "the metrical accent of poetry is subordinate
to sense") and the potential monotony of her prevailing monotone. In his discussion of the principle of modulation, where
"the great rhetorical effect" of a monotone delivery is again
affirmed, Porter cautions the student against the pitfalls of
"want of variety" and advocates the "spirit of emphasis" as the
surest remedy (pp. 47–48). One of his illustrations of the effect
of a "discriminating stress on a single word" serves as a good
example of the particular effect of the capitalization in Dickinson's verse, where the capitalized word takes precedence both
in emphasis and significance. In this illustration, Porter first
presents a couplet from Pope's "Essay on Man" as it could be
misread by ignoring the sense and by following the metrical
accent only as the guide to emphasis:

> What *the* weak head, with *strongest* bias rules.
> Is pride, the *never* failing vice of fools.

Then he says:

> Now let it be observed that in these lines there is really
> but one emphatic word, namely pride. If we mark this with
> the strong emphasis, and the falling inflection, the follow-
> ing words will of necessity be spoken as they should be,
> dropping a note or two below the key note of the sentence,
> and proceeding nearly on a monotone to the end;—thus,

What the weak head, with strongest bias rules,
Is *p*
   r
    i
     d
      e, the nēvēr fāiling vīce of fools. (pp. 50–51)

Dickinson's punctuation system would register the precise effect
Porter calls for simply by marking the word thus: "Pride ˏ",
where the falling slide would register the break of the comma as
well. The whole couplet might look like this:

> What the weak head - with strongest bias rules -
> Is Pride ˏ the never failing vice of fools.

For any poet, stress is always of primary concern, not only as
it provides the principle means of imposing his own rhythmic
patterns upon the structure of his logical base, but as leading,
or primary, stress often provides a key to meaning. In his re-
turn to the unique stress patterns of Old English verse, Gerard
Manley Hopkins found it necessary to mark leading stress with
the traditional notations, which are transcribed in all authorized
texts of his work. Because John Donne did not designate the
leading stress for the last three words in line 13 of Elegy X ("So
if I dream I have you, I have you"), two articles have been
written defending opposing positions on the proper means of
scanning the line to arrive at the poet's intention.[27] Although
many of the particular aspects of the controversy between the
"traditionalists" and the linguists over the more successful or
truer method of metrical scansion (the two-stress metrical foot

[27] See articles by Arnold Stein and Seymour Chatman in *Kenyon Review*, XVIII (1956), 439–451.

system or the phonemic four-stress isochronic distribution system) are not pertinent to an explanation of Dickinson's punctuation, it is important that such a controversy would not exist
if the poet provided the intonational signals—as her punctuation does.

The primary stress registered by Dickinson's capitalization
may either coincide with or alter the rhythms of her hymnal
meters, depending on whether the particular meaning demands
a conscious alteration of the logical base. Such alterations may
occur systematically throughout a whole poem (as will be
shown in an analysis of Poem 480), or they may be occasional,
breaking only for a particular moment the regular pattern that
is otherwise allowed to prevail. But whatever the overall metrical
pattern, Dickinson's capitalization draws attention to the word
for the significance of the word itself. Thus the negation of
"Cannot" is often emphasized, or the adjective and not the
noun ("Corporeal illustration" [Poem 709]), or the colloquial
accent will be stressed ("Half past Four" [Poem 1084]).

The punctuation of the version already quoted of "Her Grace
is all she has" promotes rather than suppresses (to use Chatman's terms) [28] the metrical framework (specifically, iambic
short meter, or two lines of six syllables followed by one of eight,
then one of six); that is, the pauses occur at the logical breaks,
and the capitalized and inflected words are the logically stressed
words:

> Her Grace is all she has,
> And that, so least displays,
> One Art, to recognize, must be,
> Another Art, to praise

A traditional scansion of the first line would place an equal
stress on "Grace," "all," and "has"; but only "Grace" receives

[28] *Ibid.*, p. 424.

primary stress; "has" is given a weaker (or "secondary") stress, and "all," a weaker still (or "tertiary"). But consider the subtle difference in meaning thus conveyed. The emphasis becomes positive, not negative; the lady has *grace,* a most praiseworthy

$$\overset{\text{s"}}{\underset{\text{a}}{}}$$

virtue *because* it is "all she h   —not the lesser virtues of beauty, wit, fame, but the "all" of "grace." It is not that "*all* in the world this poor woman *has* is *grace!*"

In a second version of this little poem, written the same year, the notation after "has" in the first line (and "displays" in the second) is a falling slide; but either inflection, without the capitalization, places less stress on this word than on the capitalized "Grace"; nevertheless, the rising slide registers at once the more precisely "gentle" tone of praise that prevails throughout the poem in the preponderance of rising slides.[29] The only other word capitalized (in both versions) is "Art," in both lines where it occurs. The limitation of the capitalization to these words implies that they are in a sense synonymous, that the delicate grace the lady "so least displays" is in itself an art.

The Punctuation and the Poetry

At one point in his discussion of emphatic inflection, Porter refers to its importance in "key-noting" meaning, and illustrates his point by suggesting that if someone's conversation were indistinctly heard from another room, the listener could determine the tone of its content, therefore something of its mean-

[29] The version quoted was sent to Sue and signed "Emily, "—the rising slide after the signature reinforcing the poem's prevailing "gentle" tone, as it was often Emily Dickinson's custom to "inflect" her signature. The other version of the poem is in packet 86 of the Bingham collection and shows not only the variants mentioned, but an elimination of the rising slide after "Art" in the third line and a concluding monotone dash. The same pattern of capitalization and a preponderance of rising slides still sustains the note of gentle praise of the first version.

ing, simply by the strength of emphasis and the particular turn of the voice with certain words. In much the same manner, Dickinson's punctuation "key-notes" meaning. The punctuation does not register every intonational distinction—for instance, there is nothing in her system that seems to denote sustained changes of pitch, or increase or decrease in volume or quantity (except as the frequency of the notations controls the timing to some degree), or such specific qualities of the voice as "plaintiveness"—but it does indicate distinctly to the eye and thus to the ear the poem's overall tone and much of its particular meaning.

The keynote of a Dickinson poem is sometimes struck immediately, as with the rising slide in the first line of the version quoted of "Her Grace is all she has, ", or with the falling slide in the first line of "Split the Lark ". But the poem's overall tone arises, not from a particular introductory inflection, but from the predominance of one notation occurring throughout. As we have said, the monotone prevails in most of the poetry, indicating not only the grave seriousness underlying the major concerns, but also, perhaps, the poet's own sensitive concern for her reader—her genuine reluctance or "fear" to "hazard" an "accent." For surely the monotone is a guarded tone (and therefore often ambiguous), for all its "sublimity, awe, and reverence," and thus may sometimes be considered a conscious device to soften or "slant" the telling of nature's "simple" news. But whatever the overall tone registered by the predominant notation, the accents and stress of the other punctuation (including, of course, the capitalization) often afford a heightened meaning not otherwise easily recognized.

For example, the whole pattern of punctuation of the fair copy of "A Bird came down the Walk -" (Poem 328) can be interpreted to reinforce the readings given the poem by two critics who have looked at it closely, at the same time that it provides some minor qualifications and a particular meaning of its own. The poem in manuscript (Bingham 98-4B-I) reads:

> A Bird came down the Walk -
> He did not know I saw -
> He bit an Angleworm in halves
> And ate the fellow,   raw,
>
> And then he drank a Dew
> From a convenient Grass ،
> And then hopped sidewise to the Wall
> To let a Beetle pass -
>
> He glanced with rapid eyes
> That hurried all around ،
> They looked like frightened Beads, I thought ،
> He stirred his Velvet Head
>
> Like One in danger, Cautious,
> I offered him a Crumb
> And he unrolled his feathers
> And rowed him softer home -
>
> Than Oars divide the Ocean,
> Too silver for a Seam ،
> Or Butterflies, off Banks of Noon
> Leap, plashless as they swim.

Charles Anderson sees the domestic setting of the garden as suggesting the possibility of a "rapprochement" with nature—a possibility which he recognizes is immediately cut off in the second line with the implication that once the poet is observed, the "make-believe of friendliness" will be at an end. "As long as the poet is unobserved, the life of nature goes on with such spontaneous informality as to give her some hope of participating in it." The rest of the poem, then, he sees as a dramatization of the difference which separates the human world from the natural world and of the impossibility of any human participation in the life of nature. "The poet is left towering above and outside, having no magical elixir like Alice in Wonderland to shrink her to a level where communication is possible." [30] In accordance with Anderson's reading, the "low" level of this miniature world is emphasized by the pattern of capitalization in the first stanza: "Bird," "Angleworm" and "Walk" are all at ground level; furthermore, the primary stress of the capitalization immediately keys the important contrast between the two worlds: "Walk" is of man's creation.

In proving that the "clues" showing the natural world to be "alien" are "planted thick," Anderson's first example is the bird's dinner, eaten "raw," where, he says, " 'raw' is an attribute set off in commas for emphasis; the human being cooks his meat and sticks to vertebrates, in general." To be sure, "raw" is set off for emphasis, but the rising slides establish the implied comparison to the manner of human eating far more conclusively than separating commas do; moreover, since a falling inflection would ordinarily register the "distress" of the observer, the rising slides, as they appear here and in the last stanzas, seem to convey a particular kind of ironic countertone. This countertone, along with the poem's prevailing singsong rhythm (the punctuation sustains the iambic short meter framework), suggests a meaning beyond the themes of separation and alienation, a theme which might be described as a deliberate reversal of the traditional romantic concept of natural observation as solace. Such a meaning would comply with Clark Griffith's interpretation of many of the poet's "childhood" poems in which the familiar romantic theme of the child "go-

[30] Charles Anderson, *Emily Dickinson's Poetry: Stairway of Surprise* (New York: Holt, Rinehart and Winston, 1960), pp. 117–119.

ing to Nature's house" for affirmation is overtly expressed in the setting and situation, but is completely undermined in the "sinister and unlovely undertones" that ultimately define the poem as one of negation. Referring specifically to "By the Sea" (Poem 520), Griffith says, "Throughout the opening two stanzas . . . Emily Dickinson appears to have imposed upon her material the same happy alliance between Nature and childhood which had begun with Blake, continued into Wordsworth, and reached its apogee in Whitman. Setting off to visit Nature . . . she strikes us as just one more romanticized urchin, who is claiming her rightful status in the natural world, and for whom, in another moment, the complexities of existence will commence to dissolve. But the moment never comes. Instead of the acceptance we have anticipated, there begins in line nine a drama of rejection which continues to the end of the poem." [31]

In "A Bird came down the Walk" there is nothing beyond the surface of the garden setting which meets the traditional expectations of the observer (as these expectations are manifest in the "gentle" voice and singing rhythm); instead she is forced to recognize not only nature's savagery and hostility, and thus her alienation, but her comparative human limitations as well. The capitalization of the second stanza provides the key to the last theme. The creatures of nature, in their "difference," are likewise entirely self-sufficient: a "Dew" is enough to quench thirst, and a "convenient Grass," not a glass, will suffice. They are also equally at home within or without the "Wall" which defines (and confines) the human world—provided, of course, the human being does not intrude. When the speaker does intrude, later in the poem, the bird simply flies swiftly and effortlessly to another "home" outside the wall. The lowly "Bee-

[31] For the complete explication, see Clark Griffith, *The Long Shadow: Emily Dickinson's Tragic Poetry* (Princeton, N.J.: Princeton University Press, 1964), pp. 17–24.

tle," who, in the last line, is allowed to "pass" almost regally
(in contrast to the speaker) anticipates the specific theme of
alienation that is emphasized and keyed by the capitalization
in the third and fourth stanzas.

James Reeves sees an identification made in these stanzas between the poet's "own timidity" and the "state of perpetual insecurity in which the bird lives." [32] Such an identification
could very well be the implication of the lack of terminal punctuation in the last line of the third stanza and the first of the
fourth. There is no notation after "Velvet Head," and the rising slides before and after "Cautious" indicate that this word
can be read as interruptive rather than terminal; that is, either
the bird or the speaker could be "Like One in danger, Cautious, ", or both, and the ambiguity of the punctuation (or
lack of it) intentional. The additional stress on "One" seems to
reinforce the double reference here, just as the strongly stressed
"Crumb" in the next line can be read with emphasis since it
symbolizes the end of the poet's futile attempts to identify with
the bird.

But I would hesitate to agree with Reeves that the predominant characteristic of the bird in this poem is "perpetual
insecurity." He is seen this way only through the eyes of the
speaker once she realizes she is intruding upon his world. That
she then begins to *force* an identification with the bird is
witnessed in the shift from the natural imagery of the opening
stanzas to her now more unnatural way of seeing. And again
the stress of the capitalization provides the key. The "rapid"
eyes of the bird are described as "frightened Beads," and his
"Head" is "Velvet." She seems to be attempting here to see

32 "Introduction," *Selected Poems of Emily Dickinson*, ed. James Reeves
(New York, 1959; London, 1959), reprinted in *Emily Dickinson: A Collec-
tion of Critical Essays*, ed. Richard B. Sewall (Englewood Cliffs, N.J.:
Prentice Hall, Inc., 1963), p. 124.

the bird in terms more specifically related to the "made" world, or the more limited area of her own understanding, just as she next seems to force a comparison between her own feelings and the bird's—"Like One in danger, Cautious, "—through the stress on "One" and the line's double reference. But with the poet's final recognition of the impossibility of rapprochement (in the offering of the "Crumb"), the natural imagery of the opening stanzas comes back into play with the flight of the bird. His leavetaking, however, like his feasting and drinking (unobserved), is hardly described as a manifestation of insecurity. His flight is easy ("softer") "rowing," and its effortlessness and speed (or "evanescence," as Charles Anderson describes it) are described in terms of the "Seam" left by "Oars" in the "Ocean" and the "plashless" "swimming" motion of "Butterflies" as they fly out of sight ("Off Banks of Noon").

The emphasis of the capitalization in the last stanza becomes the key to the merging here of all the themes and all the imagery of the preceding stanzas. In the first line the theme of separation is pointed up through the "Oars" of man's making as set against the "Ocean," and in the second line their limitation is expressly manifest in the comparatively small and very temporary "Seam" they leave as their mark. And here of course the miniature or "low" world of nature of the opening stanza is expanded to "Ocean" proportions—even though the eye is still at ground level. When it moves upward in the last lines with the "Butterflies" (and the bird's flight) this same miniature and possibly approachable world of nature is further expanded in the "Leap" (emphasized by the rising slide) beyond space ("Banks") and beyond time ("Noon") and entirely beyond man's limited reach. The miniature world is now the poet's own.

As in each of the stanzas, the poem's whole pattern of strong stress, registered by the capitalization, reinforces the major themes of separation, alienation, and limitation and suggests still another parallel theme. The capitalized words in all the stanzas, except for the very last "Banks of Noon," refer specifically to physical objects or actions, but a metaphysical emphasis is implied in this concluding capitalized phrase. In the first, second, and last stanzas, where the world of nature is witnessed in its spontaneous life before and after the poet's intrusion, the human world is still imposed upon the natural scene through the physical images of the man-made "Walk," "Wall," and the "Seam" made by the "Oars." The oars are explicitly described as "dividing," making a "Seam," and the image itself suggests man's effort to conquer time.

But so too are the walls and walks that man builds to confine space "dividing," and so too do their lines make a "Seam." In contrast, the creatures of nature do not construct such divisions (the bird's flight is "too [quick] silver for a Seam," and the butterflies' motion is "plashless"), nor are they confined by the divisions imposed by man (they can "leap" above and beyond "off Banks of Noon"), suggesting that they are not limited to or by man's distorted and distorting concepts of time and space. The theme of Emerson's "Hamatreya" is also implied through this particular pattern of the capitalization, which suggests that just as the ocean will quickly erase the oars' "Seam," so too are all man's efforts to conquer space (by walks and walls) or time (by speeding oars) equally temporary and futile.

By looking at the alterations of the punctuation from the semifinal draft to the fair copy of the poem just analyzed, we can see that Dickinson's choice of punctuation is as much a manifestation of her conscious artistry as her choice of words. The semifinal draft (in packet 85 [Bingham 32c]) reads:

A Bird, came down the Walk -
He did not know I saw -
He bit an Angle Worm in halves
And ate the fellow, raw,

And then, he drank a Dew
From a convenient Grass,
And then hopped sidewise to the Wall
To let a Beetle pass -

He glanced with rapid eyes,
That hurried all abroad -
They looked like frightened Beads, I thought,
He stirred his Velvet Head

Like one in danger, Cautious,
I offered him a Crumb,
And he unrolled his feathers
And rowed him softer Home,

Than Oars divide the Ocean,
Too silver for a Seam,
Or Butterflies, off Banks of Noon,
Leap, plashless as they swim -

["shook -" is suggested as a variant for "bit" in line three]

The only word change is in line ten, where "abroad" becomes "around" in the fair copy. This seems a relatively minor
change, and yet it suggests that in the final version the poet is
limiting the bird's spatial domain more precisely to the ground,
or to the physical landscape within the speaker's vision.
"Abroad" suggests the broader domain of his other "home,"
the implication of which is purposely withheld at this point to
emphasize the contrast later in his flight away. The suggested

change from "bit" to "shook -" in the third line is not adopted
in the final copy, "bit," I suppose, being a more "savage" action
at the same time that it is superficially more of a parallel to
the manner of human eating.

The change from "Angle Worm" to "Angleworm" also seems
minor, but making it one word rather than two seems to
strengthen the three-part primary stress pattern of the first
stanza. In line six, "Convenient" becomes capitalized in the fair
copy to stress the contrast in self-sufficiency between the poet
and the bird. In line thirteen, "One" also becomes capitalized
in the final version, emphasizing the ambiguous reference of the
whole line. The capitalized "Home" in line sixteen of the semifinal draft becomes lower case in the final copy, for, if we are
correct in reading "One" and "Cautious" as deliberately capitalized to emphasize the double reference of the line, then a
similar stress on "Home" in the same stanza could imply an
extension of the ambiguity. Without the strong stress of the
capitalization, however, "home" refers only to the bird's domain in a simple contrast to the poet's, now that there is no
longer the possibility of identification.

The notational variations are more numerous. In the first
two stanzas of the final version the elimination of the rising
slides after "Bird" and "then" allows a more uninterrupted
flow of the calculated singsong rhythm. In the third stanza the
elimination in the final copy of the rising slide after "eyes"
places less stress on the image here to emphasize later the more
unnatural comparison to "frightened Beads" (stressed in both
versions by the rising slide). The falling slide after "around" in
the final version stresses the particular "where" of the adverb
in contrast to the less specific "abroad." Similarly, the falling
slide after "I thought" places a more forcible emphasis on the
phrase than the rising slide of the first version. It is important
to know that this is the speaker's way of seeing at the particular

moment, and that her "thought" has become somewhat distorted through her own fear ("frightened Beads").

The fair copy version of the fourth stanza shows no concluding notations for the second line, indicating that it is definitely run on and that the ordinary pause before the "and" of the following line is not to be registered. Thus the spontaneity of the bird's response and the rapidity of his flight away, both of which actions are simultaneous with the offering of the "Crumb," are made specifically manifest in the hurried reading pace. The monotone dash of the final copy, which replaces the falling slide at the end of this stanza, simply further deemphasizes the stress on "home." Hearing a sustained pitch here, that is, hearing the word drawn out without a rising or falling inflection, implies a kind of wistful longing that would not otherwise be conveyed.

The falling slide after "Seam" in the last stanza, which replaces the rising slide of the semifinal draft, gives the word a more decided stress in keeping with its key function for the whole pattern of the poem's capitalization as it has been interpreted. The elimination in the final copy of the rising slide after "Noon" allows the words "Noon" and "Leap" to run together, suggesting again the rapidity of the movement described as well as the simultaneity or oneness of the "Leap" beyond space and beyond time. The final period of the fair copy implies a more conclusive emphasis to the action described than the monotone dash of the semifinal draft.

The refinements of the punctuation and capitalization patterns in many of Dickinson's revisions are just as meaningful as those described, even when the changes are few and at first glance very minor. This is not always the case, however; for instance, a fair copy sent to Higginson of Poem 1068 ("Further in Summer than the Birds") shows no difference in the capitalization pattern from that of the semifinal draft written

the same year, and the punctuation changes are so few and of
such minor significance that it is difficult to see any meaningful
refinement. The punctuation of both copies is limited (and
such limitation is exceptional) to one period concluding the
second of the four stanzas in both copies, one other period,
concluding the first stanza in the fair copy and the third stanza
in the semifinal draft, and one long monotone notation separating "Druidic" and "Difference" in the next to the last line in
the semifinal draft only.

It might be well to mention at this point that the interpretation of the capitalization in this book sometimes differs from
that of the Harvard variorum text. For instance, in line eighteen
of the fair copy of "A Bird came down the Walk," Johnson does
not read "Seam" as capitalized.[33] Even with the decided changes
in Emily Dickinson's handwriting over the years, she quite
often, in writing and printing, forms the initial letters A, C, E,
M, N, O, S, U, and W the same for the upper as for the lower
case. Because the initial letter in her handwriting is often
slightly larger than the rest in the word (and, conversely, a capital letter may be comparatively small), it is sometimes extremely difficult to determine when a word beginning with
these specific letters is meant to be capitalized. The interpretation of such questionable capitalization in this edition has been
based first on the proportionate size of the letter in relation
to the other letters in the word, and second on its size in relation
to the other capital letters in the same line or in the same poem.

To give an example, here is Poem 249 as it is transcribed in
the Harvard text:

> Wild Nights - Wild Nights!
> Were I with thee
> Wild Nights should be
> Our luxury!

[33] *Poems of Dickinson,* I, 261.

Futile - the Winds -
To a Heart in port -
Done with the Compass -
Done with the Chart!

Rowing in Eden -
Ah, the Sea!
Might I but moor - Tonight
In Thee!

The transcription of the poem is the same in this book except for the rising slide which replaces the comma in line ten,[34] and the lower-case letters for "nights," lines one and three, and "winds," line five. The variant reading of the capitalization was determined largely by the fact that the initial "n's" for "nights," in all three cases, and the "w" in "winds" are no larger than the rest of the letters in the words themselves, whereas the "W's" in "Wild" in all three instances are approximately twice the size of the other letters (and are formed differently from the "w" in "winds"). For that matter, all the capital letters for each word beginning a new line and for all the other definitely capitalized words within a line ("Heart," line six, "Compass," line seven, "Chart," line eight, "Eden," line nine, "Sea," line ten, "Tonight," line eleven, and "Thee," line twelve) are approximately twice the size of the other letters. The initial "m" in "moor," line eleven, is formed in the same manner as the "M" in the first word "might," but it, like the "n" in "nights," is no larger than the rest of the letters in the word. Johnson does not transcribe "moor" as capitalized, however.

In this poem, then, there seems to be little question about the capitalization. But if there were, a third determining factor would have to come into play—whether a strong stress on the

---

[34] *Ibid.*, p. 179. The poem in manuscript is written on lined paper, and the "comma" which Johnson transcribes after "Ah" is Dickinson's highest rising slide, placed considerably above the word ("Ah ' ").

word is indicated from the context. Any decision based upon this factor, however, would necessarily have to be tentative and open to question. With this poem such a means of determining the capitalization is not too pertinent except as a kind of proving method. But I would say that "nights" is probably not capitalized because the qualifying adjective, which in all three cases is definitely capitalized, takes emphatic precedence; moreover, "nights," uncapitalized, points up, or anticipates, the more emphatic "Tonight" in line eleven, just as the definitely uncapitalized "thee" in line two anticipates "Thee" in the last line. "Winds" and "moors" both receive a natural stress from the metrical pattern, and both certainly are significant words; but "winds" does not seem to be any more important syntactically than "port" in the following line, and "port" is not capitalized. "Moor," uncapitalized, allows a special stress, in contrast, for "Tonight," which follows immediately.

The line arrangement of some of the poems in this book will also (but seldom) differ somewhat from that of the Harvard text, and, again, it is proper to show just why the interpretation may vary from Johnson's. An analysis of Poem 480 should help to explain, not only the method of determining a line arrangement that seems to approximate more closely than Johnson's the one intended in the manuscripts, but should also show just how the punctuation can function metrically as well as meaningfully. This poem has received very little of the critical comment it deserves. In the Harvard text it reads as follows:

"Why do I love" You, Sir?
Because -
The Wind does not require the Grass
To answer - Wherefore when He pass
She cannot keep Her place.

Because He knows - and
Do not You -
And We know not -
Enough for Us
The Wisdom it be so -

The Lightning - never asked an Eye
Wherefore it shut - when He was by -
Because He knows it cannot speak -
And reasons not contained -
- Of Talk -
There be - preferred by Daintier Folk -

The Sunrise - Sir - compelleth Me -
Because He's Sunrise - and I see -
Therefore - Then -
I love Thee -

The line arrangement and punctuation of the manuscript (in packet 19 [H 104b]) are as follows:

(first leaf) (1) "Why do I love" You, Sir?

      (2) Because -

      (3) The Wind does not

      (4) require the Grass

      (5) To answer - Wherefore when

      (6) He pass

      (7) She Cannot keep Her place.

(stanza break)

      (8) Because He knows - and

      (9) Do not You -

(10) And We know not -
(11) Enough for Us
(12) The Wisdom it be so -

(stanza break)

(13) The Lightning - never asked
(14) an Eye
(15) Wherefore it shut - when
(16) He was by -
(17) Because He knows it
(18) cannot speak
(19) And reasons not contained -
(second leaf)   (20) - Of Talk -
(21) There be - preferred by Daintier
(22) Folk -

(stanza break)

(23) The Sunrise - Sir - Compelleth
(24) Me
(25) Because He's Sunrise -
(26) and I see -
(27) Therefore - Then -
(28) I love Thee -

   The short lines beginning with lower-case letters (lines four, fourteen, and eighteen) are obviously meant to be extensions of the preceding lines, but, except for the very last line, where the manuscript shows sufficient space left on the line above for at least part of this line to be joined, the other short lines beginning with capitalized words are not so easily determined as independent. Except for the next to the last line, in no instance is there space enough for even the first word of the short lines on the lines immediately above.

   Johnson has limited his choice of these questionably independent lines to those in the manuscript copy numbered 2, 9, 11, and 20. But if line nine is independent, why not line sixteen? Or, if line twenty, why not line six? Or if the one word "Because," line two, why not the one word "Me," line twenty-four? Because the first line ends with a question mark, we might assume that line two stands alone, but other of Dickinson's poems show interlinear question marks ("Brazil? He twirled a Button -", from Poem 621, for instance). The decision may be an arbitrary one, but once made, it would seem that the rest of the lines whose independence is also questionable should be arranged according to a consistent pattern. I would argue that although a broken line arrangement such as Johnson presents for this poem is definitely indicated in some of the Dickinson manuscripts (as the broken line often corresponds to a decidedly more broken pattern of punctuation and metrical variation), it is not so indicated here. The notations themselves break the lines sufficiently, and I see no reason why all the short lines, capitalized or not, should not be read as extensions, the capitalization functioning as stress signals only.

I would argue further that the irregular quotation marks in the first line provide the key to the line arrangement, just as I see them signalling the imposed metrical pattern for the whole poem. The terminal set of marks is so placed to indicate that the quoted matter does not refer to the poet's opening question, but rather to the opening lines of Elizabeth Barrett Browning's sonnet, "How do I love thee?" If we will agree that Dickinson's poem of "Why" is a direct echo (or, more precisely, a direct answer) to the older poet's "How" (as I hope to show in a moment), then we can argue that Dickinson's first two lines are meant as one to accord with the question-and-answer pattern of Mrs. Browning's opening line,

How do I love thee? Let me count the ways.

The matter can be argued either way, perhaps, but if all the short lines are read as extensions, the poem emerges in a more regular form to correspond to its decided affirmation:

> "Why do I love" You, Sir? Because -
> The Wind does not require the Grass
> To answer - Wherefore when He pass
> She Cannot keep Her place.
>
> Because He knows - and Do not You -
> And We know not - Enough for Us
> The Wisdom it be so -
>
> The Lightning - never asked an Eye
> Wherefore it shut - when He was by -
> Because He knows it cannot speak -
> And reasons not contained - Of Talk - [35]
> There be - preferred by Daintier Folk -
>
> The Sunrise - Sir - Compelleth Me -
> Because He's Sunrise - and I see -
> Therefore - Then-
> I love Thee -

In his *Interpretive Biography*, Johnson refers to this poem in the section on Emily Dickinson's prosody as an example of her "expert maneuvering," and mentions specifically the "shift from

---

[35] The initial notation shown on line twenty of the manuscript copy is a rare occurrence in the manuscripts. Because this line comes at the beginning of the second leaf, and because a similar notation concludes the line before, I read the line as definitely meant to be an extension, with a strong stress on "Of." This word would seldom be capitalized and therefore might be mistaken for the initial capitalization of an independent line unless it were preceded by a repetition of the notation which concludes the line it is meant to extend.

iambic to a trochaic beat in the final line." [36] But I wonder how, without recognizing the capitalization as a specific means of designating stress, the last line can be read as definitely trochaic.[37] Ignoring the capitalization, it seems to me the line might also be scanned as iambic, "Ī lóve Thēe," or as an anapest, "Ī lóve Thée," or a dactyl, "Í lóve Thēe." Such an argument, I suppose, could result in something resembling the Stein-Chatman controversy (referred to earlier) over the proper reading of "I have you" from Donne's Elegy. Here Stein looks at the line from the viewpoint of traditional metrical scansion and sees three possible readings. Chatman, however, looks at it as a good example of how the newer method of phonemic analysis can resolve such ambiguities. He sees only one stress pattern, based on that of natural speech intonations as determined from the oral interpretations given the line by twelve different readers. I would hesitate to agree with Chatman that even one hundred different oral interpretations actually prove the poet's intention; I would rather, since we cannot know that intention, look for the possible ambiguities.

The whole point of this digression is to emphasize the very important fact that the signalled stress of Dickinson's capitalization leaves no room for such argument. We know that her last line is trochaic. I am aware that we might know it anyway, because such a rendering seems most in keeping with the poem's meaning. Nevertheless, the particular stress and punctuation of the opening lines, which Johnson does not mention, seem to me far more significant as an example of expert maneuvering. The

[36] Thomas H. Johnson, *Emily Dickinson: An Interpretive Biography* (Cambridge, Mass.: The Belknap Press of Harvard University Press, 1955), p. 97.

[37] In the section from the *Poems of Dickinson*, entitled "Notes on the Present Text" (p. lxiii), Johnson says of the poet's capitalization, "She herself was arbitrary and inconsistent in her use of capitals; some poems use none within a line except for proper nouns; others are freighted heavily with them. Her mood dictated her choice."

"irregular" quotation marks, as we have said, immediately signal, not the direct question of the speaker—as such, the terminal marks would not interrupt as they do—but rather a
deliberate echo of Mrs. Browning's poem. Moreover, the
younger poet's shift from "How" to "Why" and from "thee"
to "You" implies immediately that her poem will take a different direction, one that emphasizes the mutual interplay of
love between two people, rather than the single emotions of
the speaker (of Mrs. Browning's poem). If we look at the
particular stress of the capitalization in the opening line and
throughout much of the poem, we can see this direction quite
clearly, as it calls attention to all the forces of interplay. But we
need first to compare the metrical patterns of the opening lines
of both poems. Mrs. Browning's reads:

> How do I love thee? Let me count the ways.

or, possibly:

> How do I love thee? Let me count the ways.

Ignoring the punctuation and capitalization, we can read
Dickinson's opening line in much the same rhythm:

> "Why do I love" You, Sir? Because -

But the pause of the rising slide and the signalled stress of the
capitalization render a different rhythm:

> "Why do I love" You, Sir? Because -

This is a conspicuous shift from the rhythm of Mrs. Browning's line, and, as such, immediately registers the essential distinction between this poem and the one that it echoes. Dickin-

son's opening line places the strong stress on "I" and "You," but Mrs. Browning's stress is on "love" (and possibly "thee"). The distinction is between the abstract concept and the concrete elements. It is the "why" of love that is important to the speaker in Dickinson's poem, who explains her understanding in metaphorically concrete terms as an emotional interplay between herself and her lover (hence the more intimate "You" in the opening question). But in Mrs. Browning's poem the concentration is upon the individual feelings of the poet, described in highly abstract and more formal terms, as a means of defining the "how" of love:

> How do I love thee? Let me count the ways.
> I love thee to the depth and breadth and height
> My soul can reach, when feeling out of sight
> For the ends of Being and ideal Grace.
> I love thee to the level of everyday's
> Most quiet need, by sun and candle-light.
> I love thee freely, as men strive for Right;
> I love thee purely, as they turn from Praise.
> I love thee with the passion put to use
> In my old griefs, and with my childhood's faith.
> I love thee with a love I seemed to lose
> With my lost saints.—I love thee with the breath,
> Smiles, tears, of all my life!—and if God choose,
> I shall but love thee better after death.[38]

In a very general comparison of the two poems, the vast spatial proportions of Mrs. Browning's love, ". . . the depth and breadth and height/ My soul can reach, when feeling out of sight/ For the ends of Being and ideal Grace" are more

[38] *The Complete Poetical Works of Elizabeth Barrett Browning* (Boston and New York: Houghton, Mifflin and Co., 1900).

concretely realized in the younger poet's metaphorical imagery. Dickinson's imagery, however, extends even further as it encompasses the grass on earth, the wind and the lightning in the atmosphere, and the sun beyond space and time. The qualities of Mrs. Browning's love run the whole gamut of "quiet," "free," "pure," "passionate," innocent ("my childhood's faith"), worldly ("with a love I seemed to lose/ With my lost saints"), and infinite ("I shall but love thee better after death"). These qualities are all beautifully transformed in Dickinson's poem into a single and singular *dual* essence as natural as the wind in the grass, as forceful as the lightning, as "compelling" as the sunrise, but beyond human understanding, beyond reason ("And We know not -"), and therefore incapable of being described in "reasonable" terms ("And reasons not contained - Of Talk -") —with the hint, it would seem, that Mrs. Browning's abstract language falls short of the mark.

This dual essence, however, can be approached metaphorically in concrete terms, and the image of the sunrise in the last stanza, toward which all the preceding natural imagery builds, suggests not only the supreme nature of the younger poet's temporal human love, but also the possibility of Mrs. Browning's infinite love. The only "felt" imagery which can finally and properly describe the far more natural emotion of Dickinson's poem is that which the sunrise "compelleth"—suggesting not only the newness, the "beginning" quality of the bond between the two lovers in time, but the possibility of an infinite bond through an ultimate unity of human and natural forces out of time.

The metrical pattern defined by the capitalization plays an important role in the poem's full meaning, especially if we read it as a deliberate shifting of emphasis from Mrs. Browning's declaration. Although the lover addressed in both poems is an

equally abstract quantity (we have no direct indication of his
feelings, even in Dickinson's poem—we simply assume his
response to be on a level with the poet's), the fundamental
quality of the love described by the younger poet is one of
mutual and natural response rather than of individual feeling
and contrived reasoning. Thus in Dickinson's poem the emphasis
upon love's interplay between "I" and "You," as it is stressed
in the opening line, is sustained throughout with the parallel
stress on the "Wind" and the "Grass," the "Lightning" and
an "Eye," the "Sunrise" and "Me," and finally "I" and "Thee"
(where the concluding "Thee" brings the echo full circle).

Against the extreme regularity of the alternating iambic eight-
and six-syllable hymnal lines which provide the poem's metrical
framework, the stress of the capitalization imposes a consistent
pattern of shifting rhythm at the crucial points of emphasis, as
the younger poet draws attention to the essential difference of
her declaration. The monotone notations sustain the tone of
grave seriousness (after the first salutary emphasis of the single
rising slide) and register the significant pauses and the heightened emotional quality of the compact phrasing—in marked
contrast to the more verbose and regular lines of Mrs. Browning's poem.

But the specific manner in which the capitalization imposes
its particular emphasis is keyed into the first line of the Dickinson poem. Because the quotation marks establish the echo, we
expect this line to follow the rhythm of its source and we begin
reading, " 'Why do I love,' " but the terminal marks interrupt
the flow. The interruption forces a stress on the following "You"
and a stronger one still on the added "Sir"—the stress here
heightened all the more by the pause of the rising slide.

We must go back, then, to the beginning to read the line as
Dickinson meant it, and the point is made: " 'Why do I love'

Yóu, Sír?" Then the rhythm shifts to the poem's basic iambic
rhythm, which prevails until "He pass" and "Her place" in the
last two lines of this stanza; and here, too, it is the reversal
of the expected which makes the point of contrast: it is not "he
páss" or "her pláce," but "Hé pass" and "Hér place." In the
second stanza the same shift occurs with "He knows" in the
first line.[39] The "Of" in "Of Talk" in line eleven turns the
phrase into an emphatic spondee, which points to still another
significant contrast: Dickinson's speaker feels that "Talk" is inadequate, specifically the abstract metaphorical talk of Mrs.
Browning's speaker—a subtle slight that is reinforced in the
next line with the capitalized "Daintier Folk." The comparative
form alludes not only to "Us" but also to the speaker of the
other poem. In the concluding stanza the rhythm shifts again
with the series of stressed words and breaking notations in the first
two lines to a pattern closely resembling the emphatic spondees
of Mrs. Browning's "bréath, smiles, tears . . . if Gód chóose";
thus the echo is sustained. But where the last line of Mrs.
Browning's poem reverts to the basic iambic structure—"Ī shall
but love thee better after death"—Dickinson's closing trochees
repeat the shifted rhythm of the opening question and sustain
her speaker's contrasting point of view to the end, where the
concluding notation expertly sustains the monotone, holding
"Thee" on the same level with "I."

The intonations of voice registered by Emily Dickinson's
punctuation and capitalization are, of course, only one aspect of
that larger voice which emerges from her poetry as the essence
of its greatness—its "particularity," as Archibald MacLeish has

[39] The signalled stress that does not enforce a rhythmic shift helps to
make a particular point, such as with "Wherefore" and "Cannot" (affirmative in this instance), lines three and four, and "Do" in line five, where
the absence of a question mark after "You" indicates that this is not a
question but a statement ("You do not"), making the point less harshly
than with the rhythm of the logical base: "Yóu do nót."

put it.[40] The voice that we hear with such dramatic, human immediacy in the lines of Emily Dickinson's poems is certainly not dependent for its mastery of tone upon the notations any more than upon any other single aspect of form. Indeed, her poetry has managed to remain "alive" and "breathing" despite the regularization of her punctuation and the revision of her lines, which, until the appearance of the Harvard text in 1955, have characterized the publication of her work. The voice of Emily Dickinson possesses an inherent quality that combines and yet transcends all matters of form, and its strength is perhaps best manifested in its persistent survival in spite of editorial mufflings. The Harvard text has sharpened that voice for us considerably, but it can be sharpened even further, I believe, through a more exact rendering of the manuscript notations. For surely these notations bring the voice even closer to us, delineating with greater clarity the "last Face" of the poet's meaning.

[40] Archibald MacLeish, Louise Bogan, and Richard Wilbur, *Emily Dickinson: Three Views* (Amherst, Mass.: Amherst College Press, 1960), p. 26.

A *Summary Explanation of the Punctuation and Capitalization as Transcribed from the Dickinson Manuscripts*

The notational system of the Dickinson manuscripts consists of seven symbols and the capital letter. The system can be easily and consistently interpreted on the basis of nineteenth-century elocutionary symbols and principles—specifically those pertaining to inflection, pause, and stress. The four "irregular" symbols in the poet's system are the four standard inflectional symbols to be found in almost any nineteenth-century elocution text. The three conventional symbols are the period, question mark, and exclamation point. Finally, there is the "irregular" use of the capital letter, where any part of speech may be capitalized.

Although it is based on elocutionary principles, Dickinson's system does not seem intended for elocutionary purposes in the narrow sense of providing directions for reading her work aloud. The distinction is important, not only in terms of the larger concept of the oral quality of language, or of voice in poetry, but more particularly in terms of Emily Dickinson's own understanding of the importance of tone as the final determinant of meaning in the process of understanding. As she expresses it, "The Ear is the last Face. We hear after we see."

From Ebenezer Porter's descriptions and explanations of the

inflectional symbols and the various attitudes or tones conveyed through the different vocal inflections, the four "irregular"
symbols in the Dickinson manuscripts can be interpreted as
follows:

(ˏ) is the rising slide, which indicates that the word it follows is heard with an upward slide. Such an intonation conveys attitudes of question, incomplete thought,
tender emotion, or something implied or insinuated.
In its standard position the rising slide appears immediately after the word that takes the inflection
(word,). It may also appear a little above the writing
line (word ˎ) or high above (word ´). The higher
the slide, the more intensive the inflection heard with
the word, or the more emphatic the attitude conveyed.

(ˎ) is the falling slide, which indicates that the word is
heard with a downward slide. This intonation conveys
such attitudes as emphatic force, authority, conclusiveness, decided affirmation, surprise, distress, disgust. The standard position for this slide is also at the
writing line (word ˎ), but it may sometimes appear
below the line, under the last letter of the word
(word). In this latter position a more intensive inflection or emphatic attitude is indicated.

(-) is the symbol for the monotone. With the monotone
there is no inflection up or down; rather, the word is
heard at a sustained pitch. The monotone suggests
attitudes of grave seriousness, elevated emotion, deliberateness, dignity, awe, reverence, and the like. The
standard position for the monotone symbol is the
same as for the grammatical dash (word -). The longer
symbol (—) indicates a longer pause.

(˘) is the circumflex. This mark indicates that the word is
heard with a turn or twist down and up, or up and

down (̡); the latter conveys the more emphatic tone. The circumflex indicates a stronger conditional, hypothetical, or ironical attitude than the rising slide.

All four symbols register a pause (like ordinary punctuation) as well as the particular inflection to be heard at the pause (much like the description of and symbols for patterns in speech recognized by the linguists as "clause terminals").

The standard symbol for the question mark registers the normal upward slide to the word it follows, as well as a definite question (just as the period registers a downward slide to the word, as well as a definite conclusion). The exclamation point registers a downward slide, plus a more emphatic note than is carried simply by the falling slide. When a question or exclamation is to be heard with other than the usual inflection, it will be marked accordingly (?), (?), (!), or (!).

The capital letter in Dickinson's system is the primary signal for the strong accent or stress in her line. Thus the interlinear capitalized word always carries a special significance, both in terms of the poem's meaning and rhythmic structure (as both are inseparable, of course). The word stressed by the capital letter will either reinforce or alter the line's basic rhythm, and thus its meaning. For example, in lines five and six of "My Life had stood - a Loaded Gun -", the altered stress on "We" in both lines signals a quite different meaning than if the stress were regularly on "roam" and "hunt." The emphasis is shifted from the particular nature of the activities to the subjects themselves, and to the fact that they are now "We" (and, possibly, that "We" are in some important respect different from ordinary hunters).

Four basic degrees of stress can be found in Dickinson's system, and these, in general, correspond to the linguists' four-stress system of metrical scansion. "Primary" stress in Dickinson's line is registered by the capitalized word; "secondary" stress by the inflected but uncapitalized word; "tertiary" stress by a word which receives the normal stress of the accentual base but is neither capitalized nor inflected, and no stress is given the word that is not capitalized, inflected, or stressed by the accentual base. Other and finer degrees of stress are registered by the underlined word, the word that is inflected as well as capitalized, and by the particular position of the inflectional notations (the higher or lower, the more stress).

The following poems are representative of the whole Dickinson canon, beginning with selections from her earliest poems and ending with her last. The poems have been selected largely on the basis of their familiarity and because altogether they illustrate the full range of her notational system. Most of them have found their way several times into anthologies or selected editions of Emily Dickinson's work.

The punctuation and capitalization follow those of the manuscripts according to the system of classification explained in the Introduction. Wherever the interpretation of any particular notation or capital letter is doubtful, a note immediately following the poem will describe the question. Except when noted otherwise, the punctuation will differ consistently from that of the Harvard text in the following manner: (1) all rising slides in all positions appear in the Harvard text as commas; (2) all falling slides, in their two positions, all monotone notations, and all circumflexes appear as conventional dashes; and (3) all exclamation points and question marks appear in their conventional forms. Any discrepancies in the interpretation of capitalization between this book and the Harvard variorum edition will also be noted. Wherever possible, the version printed is that of a fair copy of the poem, and all other extant versions are listed below it. The numbering of the poems and manuscripts follows that of the Harvard edition, and the dates of composition are those that Thomas H. Johnson has assigned to each manuscript on the basis of the poet's handwriting. Since the emphasis of this book is on the manuscript notations and capitalization, there has been no attempt to repeat most of the historical and biographical data that is fully documented in the Harvard text.

THE POEMS

89

Some things that fly there be -
Birds—Hours—the Bumblebee -
Of these no Elegy.

Some things that stay there be ,
Grief , Hills - Eternity ,
Nor this behooveth me.

There are that resting , rise.
Can I expound the skies?
How still the Riddle lies!

Manuscript: About 1859, in packet 1 (H 1b). The notation
after "Eternity," line 5, "fishtails" upward and may be intended
as a circumflex. The Harvard text shows this notation, as well
as the longer monotone notations in line 2, as a conventional
dash.

130

These are the days when Birds come back ,
A very few - a Bird or two ,
To take a backward look.

These are the days when skies resume
The old - old sophistries of June ,
A blue and gold mistake.

Oh fraud that cannot cheat the Bee ,
Almost thy plausibility
Induces my belief ,

Till ranks of seeds their witness bear ,
And softly thro' the altered air
Hurries a timid leaf.

Oh sacrament of summer days ,
Oh Last Communion in the Haze ,
Permit a child to join ,

Thy sacred emblems to partake ,
Thy consecrated bread to take
And thine immortal wine!

Manuscript: About 1859, in packet 3 (H 11a). The notations after "old," line 5, "Bee," line 7, and "bear," line 10, are
very short. "Sacrament," line 13, is capitalized in the Harvard
text, and a period appears at the end of the third and fifth
stanzas.

Other manuscripts: A second fair copy (Bingham 109–12)
was written the same year, and a third copy (Bingham 109–13)
of the first two stanzas only was written much later, about 1883.

165

A *wounded* Deer ˎ leaps highest ˎ
I've heard the Hunter tell -
'Tis but the extasy of *death* ˎ
And then the Brake is still!

The *smitten* Rock that gushes!
The *trampled* Steel that springs!
A cheek is always redder
Just where the Hectic stings!

Mirth is the mail of Anguish ˎ
In which it cautious arm ˎ
Lest anybody spy the blood
And "you're hurt" exclaim!

Manuscript: About 1860, in packet 4 (H 13a). "W*ounded*,"
line 1, "extasy," line 3, "*smitten*," line 5, "cheek," line 7, "mail,"
line 9, and "cautious arm," line 10, are all capitalized in the
Harvard text. But the initial letters, though somewhat larger
than the other letters in the words they begin, are not as large
as the initial capitals in the lines themselves and are no larger
than the initial letters in, for instance, "always," line 7, or "exclaim," line 12.

177

Ah ´ Necromancy Sweet!
Ah ´ Wizard erudite!
Teach me the skill ˎ

That I instil the pain
Surgeons assuage in vain,
Nor Herb of all the plain
Can heal!

Manuscript: About 1860, in packet 4 (H 16d).

239

"Heaven"—is what I cannot reach!
The Apple on the Tree -
Provided it do hopeless - hang -
That - "Heaven" is - to me !

The color, on the cruising cloud -
The interdicted Land -
Behind the Hill—the House behind -
There - Paradise - is found!

Her teazing Purples - Afternoons,
The credulous - decoy -
Enamored - of the Conjuror -
That spurned us - Yesterday!

Manuscript: About 1861, in packet 14 (H 71d). "Color,"
"cruising," and "cloud," line 5, may possibly be capitalized, as
they are in the Harvard text, but the "c's" are no larger than in
"cannot," line 1, and in "credulous," line 10, and are not as
large as in "Conjuror," line 11. "Me," line 4, is also capitalized
in the Harvard text, and the long monotone notations in lines
1 and 7 are shown as conventional dashes.

249

Wild nights—Wild nights!
Were I with thee
Wild nights should be
Our luxury!

Futile - the winds -
To a Heart in port -
Done with the Campass -
Done with the Chart!

Rowing in Eden—
Ah′ the Sea!
Might I but moor - Tonight -
In thee!

Manuscript: About 1861, in packet 8 (H 38b). "Nights," in lines 1 and 3, and "winds," line 5, are capitalized in the Harvard text. A discussion of the capitalization in this poem can be found in the Introduction.

252

I can wade Grief -
Whole Pools of it -
I'm used to that -
But the least push of Joy
Breaks up my feet ,
And I tip - drunken -
Let no Pebble - smile -
'Twas the new Liquor -
That was all!

Power is only Pain -
Stranded , thro' Discipline ,
Till Weights - will hang -
Give Balm - to Giants ,
And they'll wilt , like men -
Give Himmaleh -
They'll carry - Him!

Manuscript: About 1861, in packet 23 (H 126b). "Carry," in the last line, is capitalized in the Harvard text, but if the "c" here is intended as a capital, then the one in "can," line 1, must be also, for it is the same size. "New," line 8, and "men," line 14, are also capitalized in the Harvard text.

280

I felt a Funeral , in my Brain ,
And Mourners to and fro
Kept treading - treading - till it seemed
That Sense was breaking through -

And when they all were seated ,
A Service , like a Drum ,
Kept beating - beating - till I thought
My Mind was going numb -

And then I heard them lift a Box
And creak across my Soul
With those same Boots of Lead , again ,
Then Space - began to toll ,

As all the Heavens were a Bell ,
And Being , but an Ear ,
And I , and Silence , some strange Race
Wrecked , solitary , here -

And then - a Plank in Reason, broke,
And I dropped down, and down -
And hit a World, at every plunge,
And Finished knowing - then -

Manuscript: About 1861, in packet 32 (H 53c). Crosses before "plunge," line 19, and "Finished," line 20, indicate that
the words "Crash -" and "Got through -", written on one line
at the end of the poem, are suggested changes. The falling slide
after "Brain," line 1, has a slight "s" curve to it. The notation
after "then," line 17, is period size and placed closer to the following "a" than to "then." It may be only an ink blot. The
notations after "Space," line 12, "down," line 18, and "knowing," line 20, have very slight curves. The manuscript shows
"Brain," line 10, crossed out and "Soul" substituted.

311

It sifts from Leaden Sieves -
It powders all the Wood.
It fills with Alabaster Wool
The Wrinkles of the Road -

It makes an Even Face
Of Mountain, and of Plain -
Unbroken Forehead from the East
Unto the East again -

It reaches to the Fence -
It wraps it Rail by Rail
Till it is lost in Fleeces -
It deals Celestial Vail

To Stump   and Stack   and Stem
A Summer's empty Room -
Acres of Joints   where Harvests were
Recordless   but for them -

It Ruffles Wrists of Posts
As Ankles of a Queen
Then stills it's Artisans   like Ghosts -
Denying they have been

Manuscript: About 1862 (H 278). The copy is signed
"Emily -".

Other manuscripts: A semifinal draft, written earlier in the
same year, is in packet 29 (H 155a). A variant twelve-line version (Bingham 98-4B-3) was written about 1864, and in 1883,
a copy of this later version was sent to Thomas Niles (Bingham
106–32).

328

A Bird came down the Walk -
He did not know I saw -
He bit an Angleworm in halves
And ate the fellow   raw

And then he drank a Dew
From a convenient Grass
And then hopped sidewise to the Wall
To let a Beetle pass -

He glanced with rapid eyes
That hurried all around
They looked like frightened Beads   I thought
He stirred his Velvet Head

Like One in danger, Cautious,
I offered him a Crumb
And he unrolled his feathers
And rowed him softer home -

Than Oars divide the Ocean,
Too silver for a Seam,
Or Butterflies, off Banks of Noon
Leap, plashless as they swim.

Manuscript: About 1862 (Bingham 98-4B-1). The Harvard
text does not capitalize "Seam," line 18, or "One," line 13.

Other manuscripts: A semifinal draft, written earlier the same
year, is in packet 85 (Bingham 32c). A discussion of the changes
in punctuation and capitalization from this draft to the final
copy may be found in the Introduction.

338

I know that He exists.
Somewhere - in silence -
He has hid his rare life
From our gross eyes.

"Tis an instant's play -
'Tis a fond Ambush -
Just to make Bliss
Earn her own surprise!

But - should the play
Prove piercing earnest -
Should the glee - glaze -
In Death's - stiff - stare -

Would not the fun
Look too expensive!
Would not the jest -
Have crawled too far!

Manuscript: Early 1862, in packet 6 (H 24a). "Joke" is
crossed out in line 13, and "fun" substituted immediately after.
The "e's" in "exists," line 1, "eyes," line 4, "earnest," line 10,
and "expensive," line 14, are all almost large enough to be considered capitals. However, they are not as large as the "E" in
"Earn," line 8, and they are not transcribed as capitals in the
Harvard text. The rather short monotone notation at the end
of line 5 is shown as a period in the Harvard text, and "Silence,"
line 2, is capitalized.

341

After great pain, a formal feeling comes -
The Nerves sit ceremonious, like Tombs -
The stiff Heart questions 'Was it He, that bore',
And 'Yesterday, or Centuries before'?

The Feet, mechanical, go round -
A Wooden way
Of Ground, or Air, or Ought,
Regardless grown,
A Quartz contentment, like a stone -

This is the Hour of Lead -
Remembered, if outlived,
As Freezing persons, recollect the Snow -
First - Chill - then Stupor - then the letting go -

Manuscript: Early 1862, in packet 6 (H 26c). In the second
stanza the numbers 1, 3, 2, 4, underscored, appear before the

first four lines, indicating they are to be read in this order rather than in the order they appear originally, where the stanza reads as follows:

> The Feet, mechanical, go round -
> Of Ground, or Air, or Ought,
> A Wooden way
> Regardless grown,
> A Quartz contentment, like a stone -

The Harvard text does not capitalize "Was," line 3, and omits the single quotation marks in lines 3 and 4. The lines in the second stanza are arranged as they appear without the renumbering. The notation after "First," line 13, is very short, and the one after "Lead," line 10, has a slight curve.

412

I read my sentence - steadily,
Reviewed it with my eyes,
To see that I made no mistake
In it's extremest clause -
The Date, and Manner, of the shame,
And then the Pious Form
That "God have mercy" on the Soul
The Jury voted Him -
I made my soul familiar, with her extremity,
That at the last, it should not be a novel Agony,
But she, and Death, acquainted,
Meet tranquilly, as friends,
Salute, and pass, without a Hint,
And there, the Matter ends -

Manuscript: About 1862, in packet 26 (H 142b). The Harvard text does not capitalize "Manner," line 5. The notation after "Him," line 8, has a slight twist. "Eyes," line 2, "extremest," line 4, "extremity," line 9, and "ends," in the last line, may be intended as capitalized, although the Harvard text does not do so, and the initial "e's" are, as often, halfway between the capital and lower-case letter in size.

441

This is My letter to the World
That never wrote to Me -
The simple News that Nature told
With tender Majesty

Her Message is Committed
To Hands I Cannot see -
For love of Her - Sweet - Countrymen -
Judge tenderly - of Me

Manuscript: Early 1862, in packet 29 (H 70b). The Harvard text does not capitalize "Committed," line 5, "Cannot," line 6, or "Countrymen," line 7, but the "C's" are all as large or larger than the other capitals in the poem. Similarly, the Harvard text does not capitalize "My," line 1, though the "M" is the same as in "Me," line 2. The notation after "Me," line 2, has a slight twist, and that after "see," line 6, is short. The one after "Sweet," line 7, is spaced far over to the right and is low.

449

I died for Beauty, but was scarce
Adjusted in the Tomb
When One who died for Truth ′ was lain
In an adjoining Room -

He questioned softly "Why I failed"?
"For Beauty", I replied,
And I - for Truth - Themself are One -
We Bretheren, are", He said -

And so ' as Kinsmen, met a Night,
We talked between the Rooms,
Until the Moss had reached our lips,
And covered up - our names -

Manuscript: About 1862, in packet 34 (H 183c). The notation after "up" in the last line is very short. "Our" in the last
line may be capitalized.

465

I heard a Fly buzz - when I died -
The Stillness in the Room
Was like the Stillness in the Air
Between the Heaves of Storm -

The Eyes around - had wrung them dry -
And Breaths were gathering firm
For that last Onset - when the King
Be witnessed - in the Room -

I willed my Keepsakes - Signed away
What portion of me be
Assignable - and then it was
There interposed a Fly,

With Blue - uncertain - stumbling Buzz -
Between the light - and me -
And then the Windows failed - and then
I could not see to see -

Manuscript: About 1862, in packet 84 (Bingham 20c). The Harvard text omits the notation after "uncertain," line 13.

480

"Why do I love" You, Sir? Because -
The Wind does not require the Grass
To answer - Wherefore when He pass
She Cannot keep Her place.

Because He knows - and Do not You -
And We know not - Enough for Us
The Wisdom it be so -

The Lightning - never asked an Eye
Wherefore it shut - when He was by -
Because He knows it cannot speak -
And reasons not contained - Of Talk -
There be - preferred by Daintier Folk -

The Sunrise - Sir - Compelleth Me -
Because He's Sunrise - and I see -
Therefore - Then -
I love Thee -

Manuscript: About 1862, in packet 19 (H 104b). The Harvard text does not capitalize "Cannot," line 4, or "Compelleth," line 13. The differences in line arrangement between this reading and that of the Harvard text are discussed in the Introduction.

510

It was not Death, for I stood up,
And all the Dead, lie down -
It was not Night, for all the Bells
Put out their Tongues, for Noon.

It was not Frost, for on my Flesh
I felt Siroccos - crawl -
Nor Fire - for just my Marble feet
Could keep a Chancel · cool -

And yet, it tasted, like them all,
The Figures I have seen
Set orderly, for Burial ·
Reminded me, of mine -

As if my life were shaven,
And fitted to a frame,
And could not breathe without a key,
And 'twas like Midnight, some -

When everything that ticked, has stopped -
And Space stares, all around -
Or Grisly frosts, first Autumn morns,
Repeal the Beating Ground -

But, most, like Chaos - Stopless - cool -
Without a Chance, or Spar -
Or even a Report of Land,
To justify - Despair.

Manuscript: Early 1862, in packet 85 (Bingham 31a). Two
variants are indicated:

5. Flesh] Knees   7. my] two

The falling slide after "Land," in the next to the last line, is higher than standard. The Harvard text omits the notation after "stares," line 18.

512

The Soul has Bandaged moments,
When too appalled to stir,
She feels some ghastly Fright come up
And stop to look at her -

Salute her, with long fingers,
Caress her freezing hair,
Sip, Goblin, from the very lips
The Lover - hovered - o'er -
Unworthy, that a thought so mean
Accost a Theme - so - fair -

The soul has moments of Escape,
When bursting all the doors -
She dances like a Bomb, abroad,
And swings upon the Hours,

As do the Bee - delirious borne,
Long Dungeoned from his Rose,
Touch Liberty - then know no more,
but Noon, and Paradise -

The Soul's retaken moments,
When, Felon led along,
With shackles on the plumed feet,
And staples, in the Song,

The Horror welcomes her, again,
These, are not brayed of Tongue -

Manuscript: About 1862, in packet 85 (Bingham 33a). Two suggested changes are indicated:

21. shackles] irons -   22. staples] rivets -

The Harvard text shows a conventional dash instead of the usual comma for the rising slide after "her," line 5, and a comma instead of the usual dash for the falling slide after "more," line 17.

520

I started early - Took my Dog -
And visited the Sea -
The Mermaids in the Basement
Came out to look at me -

And Frigates - in the Upper Floor
Extended Hempen Hands -
Presuming Me to be a Mouse -
Aground - upon the Sands -

But no Man moved Me - till the Tide
Went past my simple Shoe ,
And past my Apron , and my Belt
And past my Boddice - too -

And made as He would eat me up -
As wholly as a Dew
Upon a Dandelion's Sleeve -
And then - I started - too -

And He - He followed - close behind -
I felt His Silver Heel
Upon my Ancle - Then My Shoes
Would overflow with Pearl -

Until We met the Solid Town -
No One He seemed to know -
And bowing - with a Mighty look ,
At Me - the Sea withdrew -

Manuscript: About 1862, in packet 5 (H 382a). Three suggested changes are indicated:

12. Boddice] Bosom/ Buckle   22. one] man -

The Harvard text capitalizes "early," line 1, but not "My," line 19.

621

I asked no other thing -
No other - was denied -
I offered Being - for it -
The Mighty Merchant sneered -

Brazil ? He twirled a Button -
Without a glance my way -
"But - Madam - is there nothing else -
That We can show - Today"?

Manuscript: About 1862, in packet 40 (H 215d). The word "smiled -" appears at the end of the poem as a variant for "sneered -" in line 4.

709

Publication - is the Auction
Of the Mind of Man -
Poverty - be justifying
For so foul a thing

Possibly - but We - would rather
From Our Garret go
White - Unto the White Creator
Than invest - Our Snow -

Thought belong to Him who gave it -
Then - to Him Who bear
It's Corporeal illustration - Sell
The Royal Air -

In the Parcel - Be the Merchant
Of the Heavenly Grace -
But reduce no Human Spirit
To Disgrace of Price -

Manuscript: About 1863, in packet 12 (H 59b).

712

Because I could not stop for Death -
He kindly stopped for me -
The Carriage held but just Ourselves,
And Immortality.

We slowly drove - He knew no haste
And I had put away
My labor and my leisure too '
For His Civility -

We passed the School, where Children strove
At Recess - in the Ring -
We passed the Fields of Gazing Grain -
We passed the Setting Sun,

Or rather - He passed Us,
The Dews drew quivering and chill -
For Only Gossamer ، My Gown ﹀
My Tippet - only Tulle -

We paused before a House that seemed
A Swelling of the Ground -
The Roof was scarcely visible -
The Cornice - in the Ground -

Since then - 'tis Centuries ، and yet
Feels shorter than the Day
I first surmised the Horses Heads
Were toward Eternity -

Manuscript: About 1863, in packet 31 (H 165a). The Harvard text does not capitalize "Only" or "My," line 15. The notation after "Civility," line 8, is very short.

754

My Life had stood - a Loaded Gun -
In Corners - till a Day
The Owner passed - identified -
And carried Me away -

And now We roam in Sovreign Woods -
And now We hunt the Doe -
And every time I speak for Him
The Mountains straight reply -

And do I smile, such cordial light
Upon the Valley glow -
It is as a Vesuvian face
Had let it's pleasure through -

And when at Night, Our good Day done -
I guard My Master's Head,
'Tis better than the Eider-Duck's
Deep Pillow - to have shared -

To foe of His - I'm deadly foe -
None stir the second time -
On whom I lay a Yellow Eye,
Or An Emphatic Thumb -

Though I than He - may longer live
He longer must - than I -
For I have but the power to kill ⸗
Without - the power to die -

Manuscript: About 1863, in packet 24 (H 131a). Four variants are listed at the end of the poem:

> 5. in] the -   18. stir] harm
> 16. Deep] low   23. power] art

The Harvard text does not capitalize "An Emphatic," line 20. The notations after "shared," line 16, and "die," in the last line, have slight downward slants. The notation after "I," line 22, is very short.

810

Her Grace is all she has,
And that, so least displays,
One Art, to recognize, must be,
Another Art, to praise

Manuscript: About 1864, a penciled copy (H 264) sent to
Sue and signed "Emily·". The Harvard text does not capitalize
"Art," line 3, and shows a dash concluding the poem, where no
notation appears in the manuscript.

Other manuscripts: Another fair copy, written the same year,
is in packet 86 (Bingham 36f).

861

Split the Lark, and you'll find the Music -
Bulb after Bulb, in Silver rolled -
Scantily dealt to the Summer Morning
Saved for your Ear when Lutes be old -

Loose the Flood - you shall find it patent,
Gush after Gush, reserved for you -
Scarlet Experiment! Sceptic Thomas!
Now· do you doubt that your Bird was true?

Manuscript: About 1864, in packet 87 (Bingham 41c). The
Harvard text shows a period concluding the first stanza.

986

A narrow Fellow in the Grass
Occasionally rides -
You may have met Him - did you not
His notice sudden is -

The Grass divides as with a Comb -
A spotted shaft is seen -
And then it closes at your feet
And opens further on -

He likes a Boggy Acre
A Floor too cool for Corn
Yet when a Boy, and Barefoot,
I more than once at Noon
Have passed, I thought, a Whip lash
Unbraiding in the Sun
When stooping to secure it
It wrinkled, and was gone -

Several of Nature's People
I know, and they know me -
I feel for them a transport
Of Cordiality,

But never met this Fellow
Attended, or alone
Without a tighter breathing
And Zero at the Bone,

Manuscript: About 1865, in packet 88 (Bingham 53a). "Cordiality," line 20, is not capitalized in the Harvard text, and the notation supplied there after "Corn," line 10, does not appear in the manuscript. The falling slide after "Bone" in the last line is placed higher than standard.

Other manuscripts: Another fair copy (H B 193) was written in 1872 and sent to Sue.

1052

I never saw a Moor -
I never saw the Sea -
Yet know I how the Heather looks
And what a Billow be -

I never spoke with God
Nor visited in Heaven -
Yet certain am I of the spot
As if the Checks were given -

Manuscript: About 1865 (Bingham 98-3-14). The notation after "be," line 4, is short, and is transcribed as a period in the Harvard text.

1068

Further in Summer than the Birds
Pathetic from the Grass
A minor Nation celebrates
It's unobstrusive Mass

No Ordinance be seen
So gradual the Grace
A pensive Custom it becomes
Enlarging Loneliness.

Antiquest felt at Noon
When August burning low
Arise this spectral Canticle
Repose to typify.

Remit as yet no Grace
No Furrow on the Glow
Yet a Druidic—Difference
Enhances Nature now

Manuscript: About 1866 (Bingham 109-3). The Harvard text shows a conventional dash in line 15.

Other manuscripts: Another fair copy (BPL Higg 13) was sent to T. W. Higginson in the same year, and still another (Bingham 106) was enclosed in a letter to Thomas Niles in 1883.

1072

Title divine, is mine.
The Wife without the Sign,
Acute Degree conferred on me -
Empress of Calvary -
Royal, all but the Crown -
Betrothed, without the Swoon
God gives us Women,
When You hold Garnet to Garnet -
Gold - to Gold -
Born - Bridalled, Shrouded -
In a Day -
Tri Victory -
"My Husband", Women say
Stroking the Melody
Is this the Way,

Manuscript: About 1866 (H 361), signed "Emily," and sent to Sue. The notations after the first "Gold," line 9, "Shrouded," line 10, and "Victory," line 12, have slight downward slants. The Harvard text shows a period concluding line 2.

Other manuscripts: An earlier copy (Bingham) was written about 1862.

1084

At Half past Three, a single Bird
Unto a silent Sky
Propounded but a single term
Of cautious melody.

At Half past Four, Experiment
Had subjugated test
And lo´ Her silver Principle
Supplanted all the rest -

At Half past Seven, Element
Nor Implement, be seen,
And Place was where the Presence was
Circumference between.

Manuscript: About 1866, in packet 35 (H 191a). The notations concluding stanzas 1 and 3 could be interpreted as monotone notations. The Harvard text shows periods concluding all
three stanzas.

Other manuscripts: Three other copies were written the same
year. One (H H 97) was sent to Dr. Holland, another (Bingham) went to an unidentified recipient, and a third is numbered Bingham 98-4B-5.

1463

A Route of Evanescence
With a revolving Wheel
A Resonance of Emerald
A Rush of Cochineal
And every Blossom on the Bush
Adjusts it's tumbled Head -
The Mail from Tunis, probably,
An easy Morning's Ride.

Manuscript: About 1879 (Bingham 99-3), presumably sent to Helen Hunt Jackson.

Other manuscripts: Four other fair copies are extant, all sent to correspondents: one (Amherst), written about 1880, to Mrs. Edward Tuckerman, and another (BPL Higg 46) to T. W. Higginson, in November 1880. Late in the same year, Dickinson sent still another copy (Bingham) to Mable Loomis Todd, and a fifth (Bingham 106) was sent to Thomas Niles about April 1883. A sixth copy, now lost, was sent to the Norcross sisters.

1551

Those - dying then,
Knew where they went -
They went to God's Right Hand -
That Hand is amputated now
And God cannot be found -

The abdication of Belief
Makes the Behavior small -
Better an ignis fatuus
Than no illume at all -

Manuscript: About 1882 (Bingham 98-1-11).

1554

"Go tell it" - What a Message -
To whom - is specified -
Not Murmur - not endearment -
But simply - we - obeyed -
Obeyed a Lure - a Longing?
Oh Nature - none of this -
To Law - said Sweet Thermopylae
I give my dying Kiss -

Manuscript: About 1882 (Bingham 107-24), written on a scrap of paper, with three suggested changes (the first simply a respelling):

> 7. Thermopylae] Thermopolae
> 8. I give] I send -
> 8] Convey my dying Kiss -

"Murmur," line 3, and "Sweet," line 7, are not capitalized in the Harvard text, and the notation supplied there after "Obeyed," line 5, does not appear in the manuscript. The notation after "Lure," line 5, has a slight downward slant.

1587

He ate and drank the precious Words -
His Spirit grew robust -
He knew no more that he was poor,
Nor that his frame was Dust -

He danced along the dingy Days
And this Bequest of Wings
Was but a Book ˎ What Liberty
A loosened spirit brings -

Manuscript: About 1883 (Bingham 98-310), written on a half sheet of a discarded letter. "The" is a suggested variant for "A," line 8.

Bibliography

Primary Sources

Poems by Emily Dickinson. Edited by Mabel Loomis Todd and T. W. Higginson. Boston: Roberts Brothers, 1891.

Poems by Emily Dickinson. Second Series. Edited by T. W. Higginson and Mabel Loomis Todd. Boston: Roberts Brothers, 1892.

The Letters of Emily Dickinson. 3 vols. Edited by Thomas H. Johnson and Theodora Ward. Cambridge, Mass.: The Belknap Press of Harvard University Press, 1965.

The Poems of Emily Dickinson. 3 vols. Edited by Thomas H. Johnson. Cambridge, Mass.: The Belknap Press of Harvard University Press, 1958.

Porter, Ebenezer. *The Rhetorical Reader*. New York: Mark H. Newman, 1835.

Secondary Sources

Allen, Donald (ed.). *The New American Poetry*. New York: Grove Press, 1960.

Anderson, Charles. *Emily Dickinson's Poetry: Stairway of Surprise*. New York: Holt, Rinehart and Winston, 1960.

Bell, Alexander M. *Principles of Elocution*. Salem, Mass.: J. P. Burbank, 1878.

Bianchi, Martha Dickinson. *Emily Dickinson Face to Face*. Boston and New York: Houghton Mifflin Company, 1932.

Bingham, Millicent Todd. *Ancestor's Brocades: The Literary Debut of Emily Dickinson*. New York and London: Harper and Brothers Publishers, 1945.

Blackmur, R. P. "Emily Dickinson's Notation," *The Kenyon Review*, XVIII (Spring 1956), 224–237.

Blake, Caesar R. and C. F. Wells (eds.). *The Recognition of Emily Dickinson: Selected Criticism Since 1890*. Ann Arbor: University of Michigan Press, 1964.

Brooks, Cleanth, and Robert Penn Warren. *Understanding Poetry*. New York: Henry Holt and Company, 1938.

Capps, Jack L. *Emily Dickinson's Reading: 1836–1886*. Cambridge, Mass.: Harvard University Press, 1966.

Chase, Richard. *Emily Dickinson*. New York: Dell Publishing Co., Inc., 1965.

Chatman, Seymour. "Robert Frost's 'Mowing': An Inquiry into Prosodic Structure," *The Kenyon Review*, XVIII (Summer 1956), 421–438.

——. "Mr. Stein on Donne," *The Kenyon Review*, XVIII (Summer 1956), 443–451.

Ciardi, John. *How Does a Poem Mean?* Boston: Houghton Mifflin Company, 1959.

Davis, Thomas M. (ed.). *14 by Emily Dickinson*. Chicago: Scott, Foresman and Co., 1964.

Drew, Elizabeth. *Poetry: A Modern Guide to its Understanding and Enjoyment*. New York: Dell Publishing Co., Inc., 1961.

Ford, Thomas W. *Heaven Beguiles the Tired: Death in the Poetry of Emily Dickinson*. University, Alabama: University of Alabama Press, 1966.

Franklin, R. W. *The Editing of Emily Dickinson: A Reconsideration*. Madison, Milwaukee, and London: University of Wisconsin Press, 1967.

Frye, Northrop (ed.). "Emily Dickinson," *Major Writers of America*, II. New York: Harcourt, Brace and World, Inc., 1962.

Gelpi, Albert J. *Emily Dickinson: The Mind of the Poet*. Cambridge, Mass.: Harvard University Press, 1965.

Gibson, William M. and George Arms. *Twelve American Writers*. New York: The Macmillan Company, 1962.

Gleason, H. A. *An Introduction to Descriptive Linguistics*. New York: Holt, Rinehart and Winston, 1961.

Griffith, Clark. *The Long Shadow: Emily Dickinson's Tragic Poetry*. Princeton, N.J.: Princeton University Press, 1964.

Higgins, David James Monroe. *Portrait of Emily Dickinson: The Poet and her Prose*. New Brunswick, N.J.: Rutgers University Press, 1967.

Higginson, T. W. "Letter to a Young Contributor," *Atlantic Monthly*, IX (April 1862), 401–411.

Howard, William. "Dickinson's 'I Never Saw a Moor,' " *The Explicator*, XXI, Item 13 (October 1962).

Johnson, Clifton. *Old Time Schools and School Books*. New York and London: The Macmillan Company, 1904.

Johnson, Thomas H. *Emily Dickinson: An Interpretive Biography*.

Cambridge, Mass.: The Belknap Press of Harvard University Press, 1955.

Leyda, Jay. *The Years and Hours of Emily Dickinson*. 2 vols. New Haven: Yale University Press, 1960.

Lindberg, Brita. "Emily Dickinson's Punctuation," *Studia Neophilologica*, XXXVII (1965), 327–359.

Lindberg-Seyersted, Brita. *The Voice of the Poet*. Cambridge, Mass.: Harvard University Press, 1968.

McGuffey, William. *Sixth Eclectic Reader*. New York: The New American Library of World Literature, Inc., 1963.

MacLeish, Archibald, Louise Bogan, and Richard Wilbur. *Emily Dickinson: Three Views*. Amherst, Mass.: Amherst College Press, 1960.

Matthiessen, F. O. "The Problem of the Private Poet," *The Kenyon Review*, VII (Autumn 1945), 584–597.

Millor, Ruth. *The Poetry of Emily Dickinson*. Middletown, Conn.: Wesleyan University Press, 1968.

Pickard, John B. *Emily Dickinson: An Introduction and Interpretation*. New York: Holt, Rinehart and Winston, 1967.

Porter, David T. *The Art of Emily Dickinson's Early Poetry*. Cambridge, Mass.: Harvard University Press, 1966.

Ransom, John Crowe, "Emily Dickinson: A Poet Restored," *Perspectives USA*, XV (Spring 1956), 5–20.

——. "The Strange Music of English Verse," *The Kenyon Review*, XVIII (Summer 1956), 460–477.

Rosenbaum, Stanford Patrick. *A Concordance to the Poems of Emily Dickinson*. Ithaca, N.Y.: Cornell University Press, 1964.

Sewall, Richard B. (ed.). *Emily Dickinson: A Collection of Critical Essays*. Englewood Cliffs, N.J.: Prentice Hall, Inc., 1963.

Sherwood, William R. *Circumference and Circumstance: Stages in the Mind and Art of Emily Dickinson*. New York: Columbia University Press, 1968.

Stamm, Edith Perry. "Emily Dickinson: Poetry and Punctuation," *Saturday Review*, XLVI (March 30, 1963), 26–27, 74.

——. Letter to the Editor, *Saturday Review*, XLVI (May 25, 1963), 23.

Stein, Arnold. "A Note on Meter," *The Kenyon Review*, XVIII (Summer 1956), 451–460.

——. "Donne's Prosody," *The Kenyon Review*, XVIII (Summer 1956), 439–443.

Taggard, Genevieve. *The Life and Mind of Emily Dickinson*. New York: Knopf, 1930.

Tate, Allen. *On the Limits of Poetry*. New York: The Swallow Press and William Morrow and Company, 1948.

Tuckerman, Frederick. *Amherst Academy*. Amherst, Mass.: Printed for the Trustees, 1929.

Ward, Theodora. Letter to the Editor, *Saturday Review*, XLVI (April 27, 1963), 25.

——. *The Capsule of the Mind*. Cambridge, Mass.: Harvard University Press, 1961.

Warren, Austin. "Emily Dickinson," *Sewanee Review*, LXV (Autumn 1957), 565–586.

Wells, Anna Mary. *Dear Preceptor: The Life and Times of Thomas Wentworth Higginson*. Boston: Houghton Mifflin Company, 1963.

Wells, Henry W. *Introduction to Emily Dickinson*. Chicago: Packard and Company, 1947.

Whicher, George Frisbie. *This Was a Poet*. Ann Arbor: University of Michigan Press, 1957.

Whicher, Stephen E. (ed.). *Selections from Ralph Waldo Emerson*. Boston: Houghton Mifflin Company, 1960.

Whitehall, Harold. "From Linguistics to Criticism," *The Kenyon Review*, XVIII (Summer 1956), 411–421.

——. *Structural Essentials of English*. New York: Harcourt, Brace and World, Inc., 1956.

Index
of First Lines of Poems